Australian Beaks

BIRD COLOURING JOURNAL

Shelley May Kurtz

For Maui.
The little Sun Conure parrot
that inspired this book.

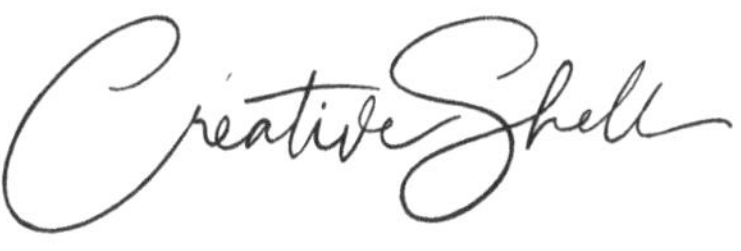

Introduction

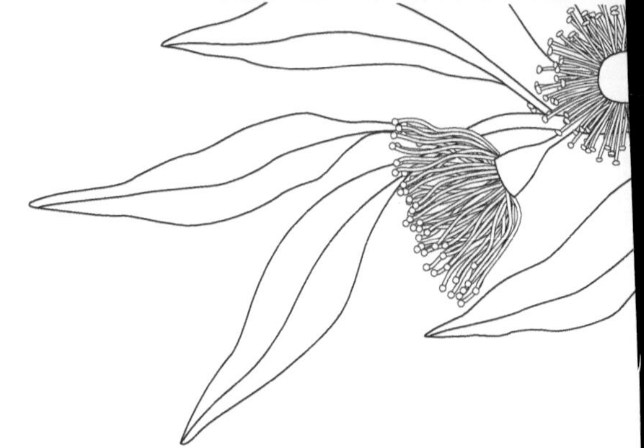

Welcome to Australian Beaks!

This bird colouring journal is a great way to appreciate how beautiful, unique, and delightful our feathered friends are. Whether you are a passionate birder, a nature lover, or just enjoy colouring, this book allows you to explore the fascinating world of birds in a creative and engaging way.

Inside this journal, you will find unique illustrations of common backyard birds and rare species only found in small areas of Australia. Their simplicity allows you to add your own colours and species variations. Get creative and add your own backgrounds and habitats to surround the birds.

Each Australian bird comes with its own information page and bird journal, so you can learn about them as you bring the illustrations to life and record your observations and experiences. If you cannot find a certain species in your area, visit your nearby zoo, you might find them there. Alternatively, you can look for similar species that are found in your area instead.

Your journal also includes blank spaces for you to draw your own bird sightings or birds you would love to see. You may have already noticed the colour references on the inside front cover for all the birds featured. If you would rather come up with your own colours, that's fine too.

There's a blotting page at the back of the book. Cut this out and place it under the page you're colouring and it will help prevent pens and markers from bleeding through onto other pages.

This colouring journal is not only a fun and relaxing activity, but also a valuable tool for bird enthusiasts of all levels. By colouring and learning about Australian birds, you can develop your observation skills, expand your knowledge of natural history, and connect with the natural world around you.

I hope my illustrations encourage and inspire you to explore your own creative side and come out of your creative shell.

So, grab your coloured pencils, pens and markers and get ready to embark on a colourful journey through the world of Australian birds!

Australian Beaks
Bird Colouring Journal © Creative Shell 2023
Illustrations © Creative Shell 2023
www.creativeshell.com.au

Printed and bound in Australia by IngramSpark.

ISBN: 978-0-646-87264-3

Share your creations on social media
#australianbeaks

 the.creative.shell
 creativeshell

Disclaimer
The information in this book was deemed accurate at the time of publication. The author cannot be held responsible for any errors or changes that may have occurred since printing.

Acknowledgments
This book would not have been possible without the help and encouragement from those around me. To my parents, thank you for always supporting my dreams from a young age. Mum, thank you for being my number one supporter. Grandpa, thank you for encouraging me to draw. I'll be using the Derwent pencils you bought me when I was ten to colour this with. Thank you to my partner Reece, my friends Louise and Kellie - you were all there, supporting me every step of the way. Aunty Nerida, thank you for your invaluable contribution in proofreading this book. Lastly, if you are reading this, thank you for colouring this book and supporting a small Australian business.

This book belongs to

My favourite
Australian bird is

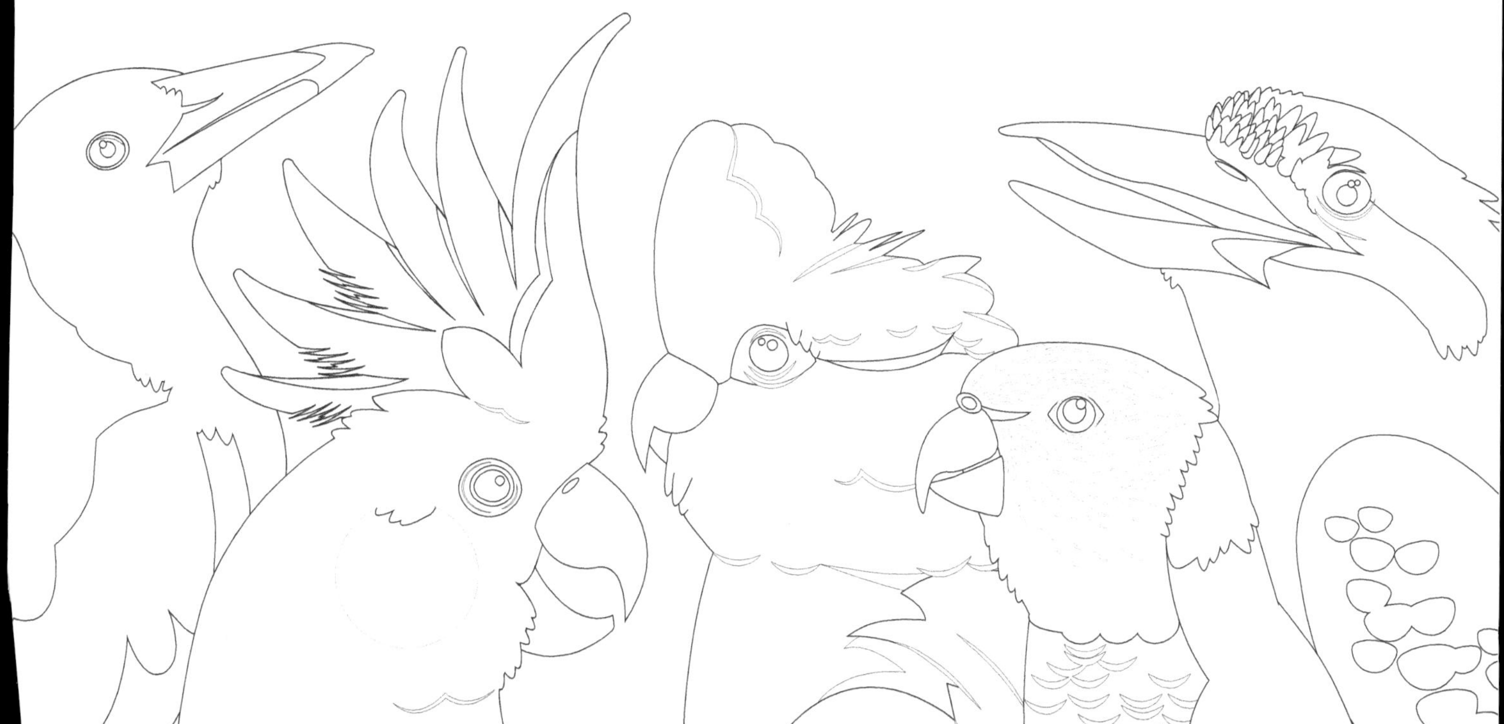

Rainbow *Bee-eater*

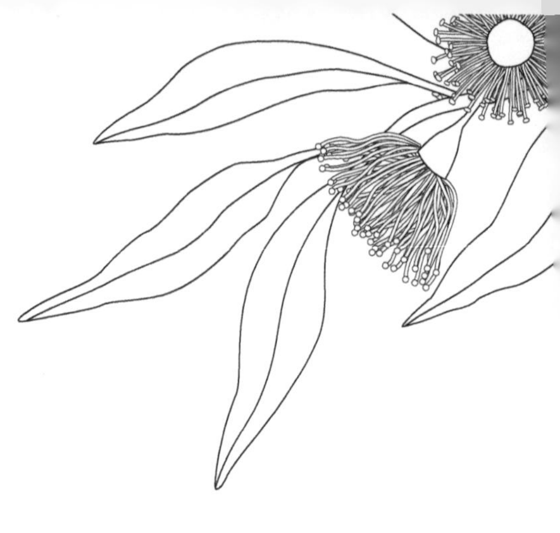

Rainbow Bee-eaters have long, curved beaks which they use to catch insects in mid-air. They rub bees and wasps against tree branches to remove the stingers and venom glands so they don't get stung or poisoned while eating them.

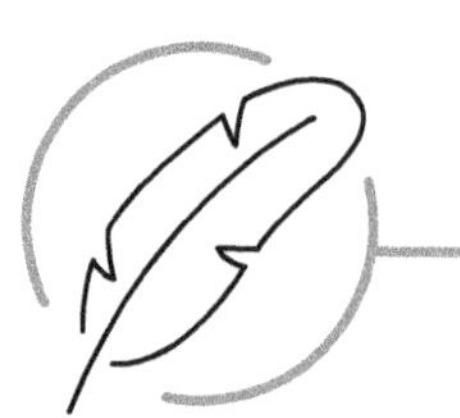

Identification

Rainbow Bee-eaters are vibrant and known for their slim, curved beaks and long black-blue tails with unique tail-streamers. They have golden heads with red eyes inside a black stripe that extends from their beaks to their ears. A blue line underlines the stripe. A thick black band separates their golden heads from their green and blue bodies. Their wings are green, with copper black- tipped flight feathers. Their underwings are bright orange.

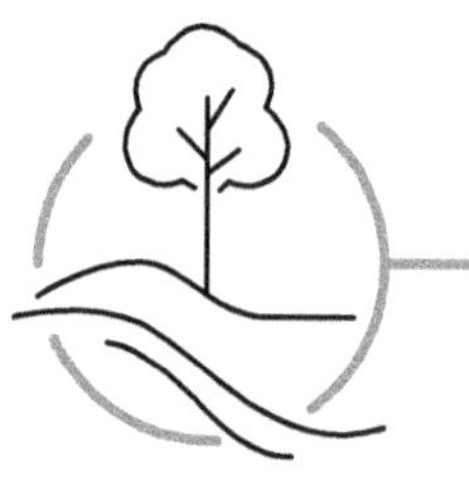

Habitat

Rainbow Bee-eaters can be found in a wide range of habitats. They prefer open woodlands, savannahs, and forests that have a mix of both open areas and trees. They are found near water, such as rivers, lakes, and wetlands, where they can find suitable nesting sites and forage for insects.

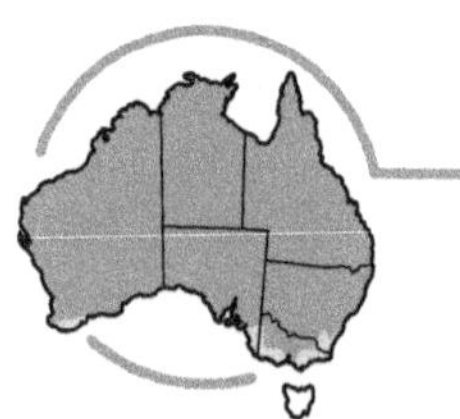

Distribution

Rainbow Bee-eaters are found across much of mainland Australia. They are found in higher numbers along the eastern and northern coasts of Australia.

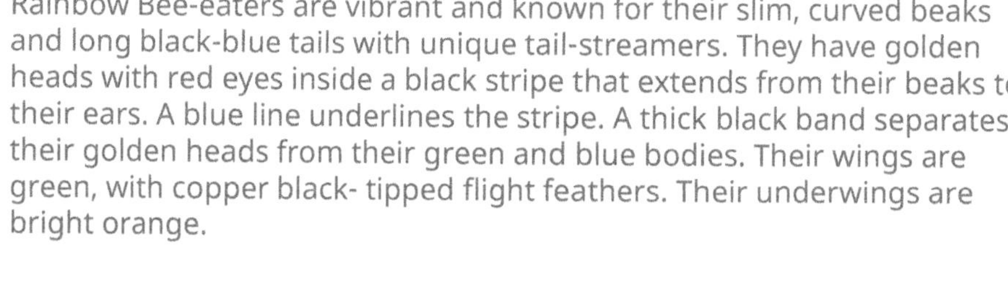

Bird Journal

Date seen: _______________________ Time seen: _______________________

Location: ____

Observations: ____

____

____

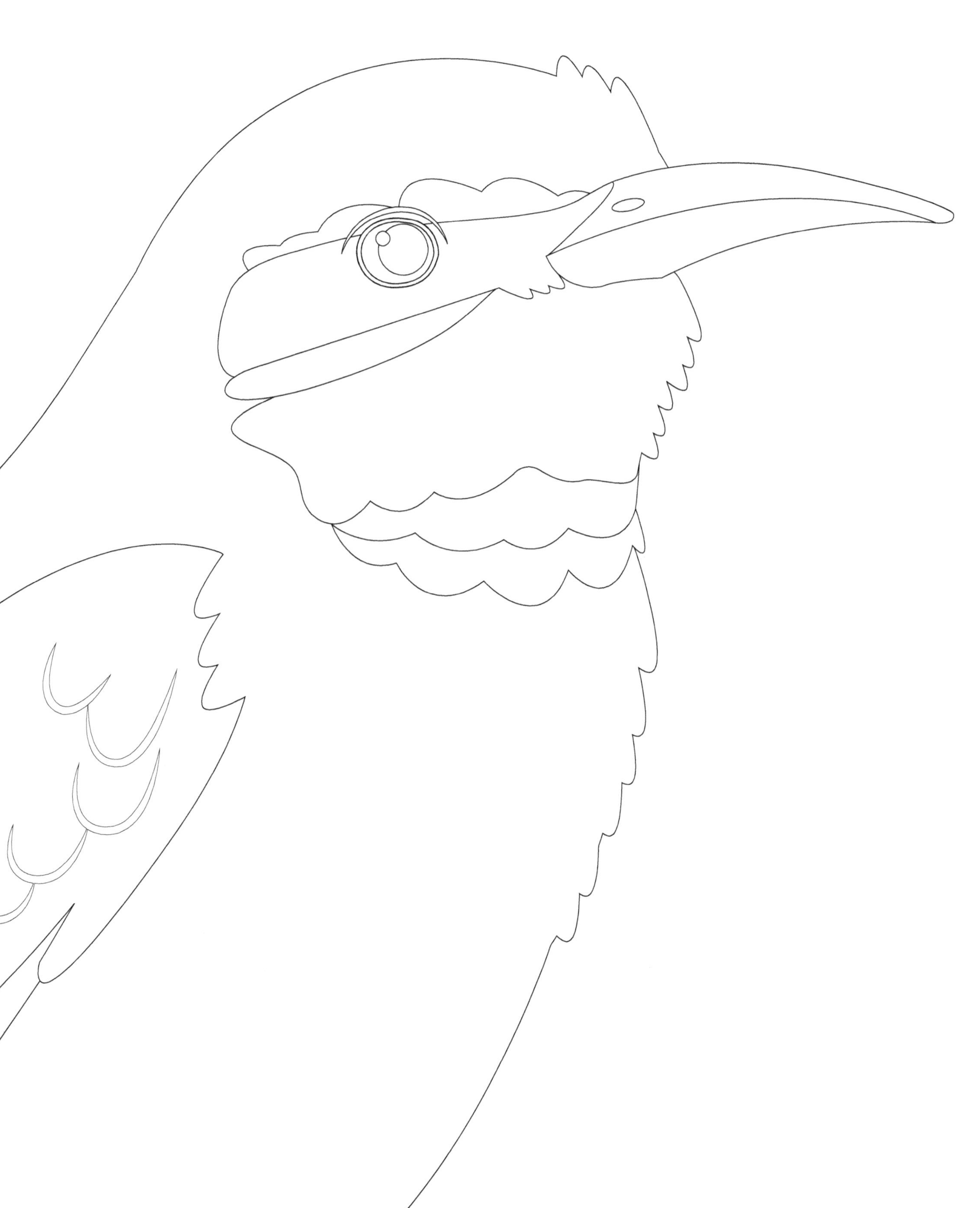

Budgerigar

Budgerigars are more commonly known as Budgies. Budgies have bright green and yellow feathers, which helps them to blend into their natural environment. They are popular as pets around the world and have been bred in captivity into a variety of colours, including blues, whites, yellows, mauves, and greys.

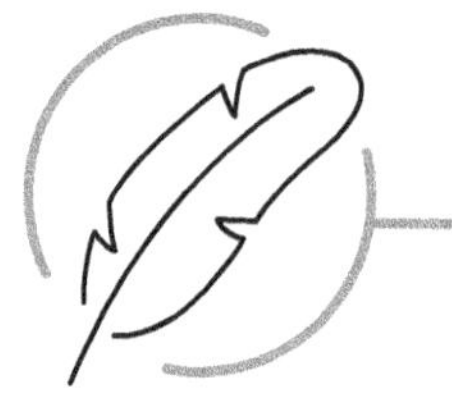

Identification

In the wild, Budgies have mainly green feathers, with yellow feathers on their foreheads, faces, and chests. They have black scalloped markings on their backs, wings, and necks, with a small blue patch on their cheeks and black spots around the bottom of their throats. Budgie's genders are shown by the colour of their cere, which is the area surrounding their nostrils. Males have a dark blue cere, while females have a pale blue one, which changes to pinkish-brown when they mature.

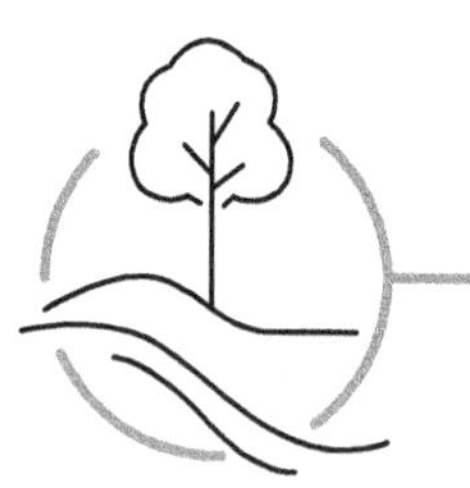

Habitat

Wild Budgies are found in drier parts of Australia. They adapt well to the harsh Australian environment and can be found in different habitats, such as open grasslands, woodlands, deserts, and scrublands. These social birds have an average flock size ranging from three to 100 birds, often gathering around water. After rainfall, their numbers can increase, with flocks reaching tens of thousands.

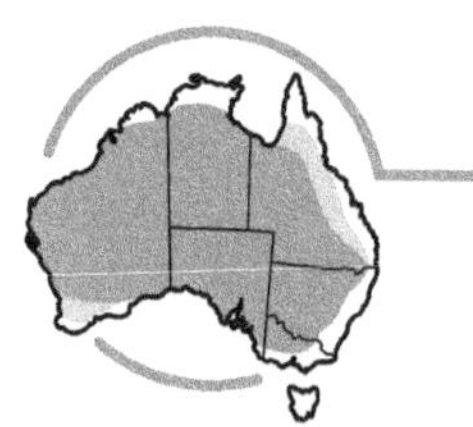

Distribution

Budgies are found throughout most of Australia, except for the coastal areas in the far north and south-east. They are widespread in the arid and semi-arid regions of Australia.

Date seen: **Time seen:**

Location:

Observations:

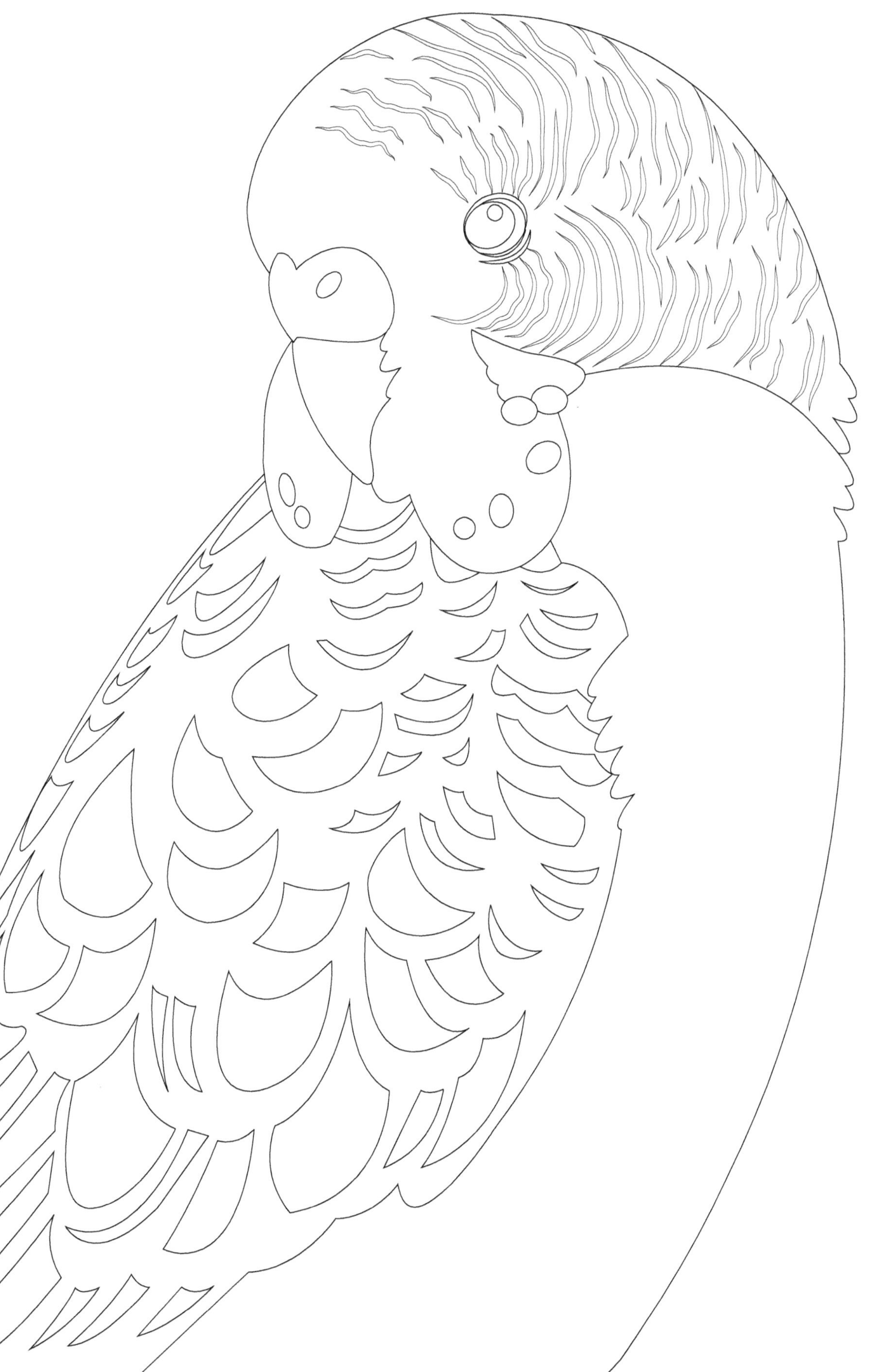

Southern Cassowary

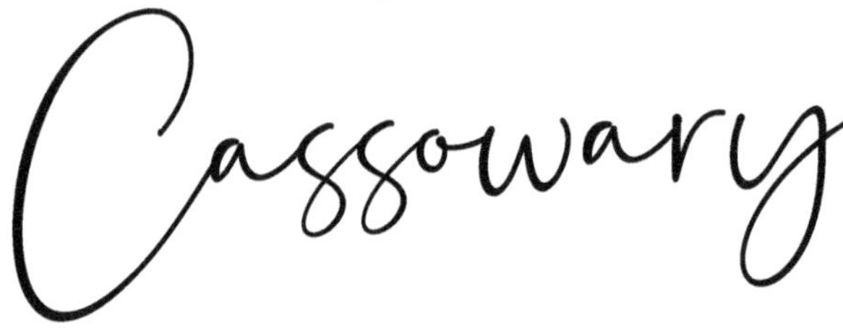

The Southern Cassowary is one of the largest birds in the world. It can grow up to 1.8 metres tall and weigh up to 65kg. Despite their large size, Southern Cassowaries are shy birds. However, they are territorial and will aggressively defend their space if they feel threatened.

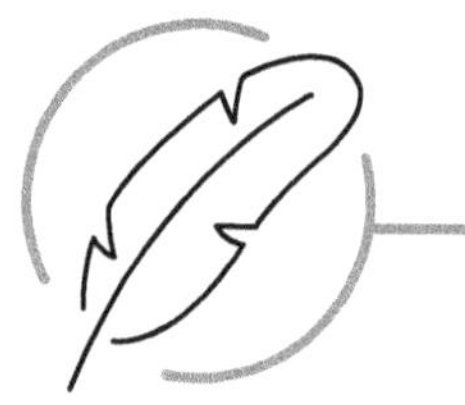

Identification

Southern Cassowaries have a unique appearance. They have a tall, slender body with long legs, shiny black feathers and distinctive, horn-like casques on their heads which are believed to be used for both communication and defence. The bare skin on their faces and necks is bright blue with a pink-purple hind-neck. Two long, thin reddish-pink wattles hang from the front of their necks. Their legs are strong and powerful, allowing them to move through dense forests. Cassowaries have three-toed feet, with the middle toe carrying a long, sharp claw that can be used for self-defence.

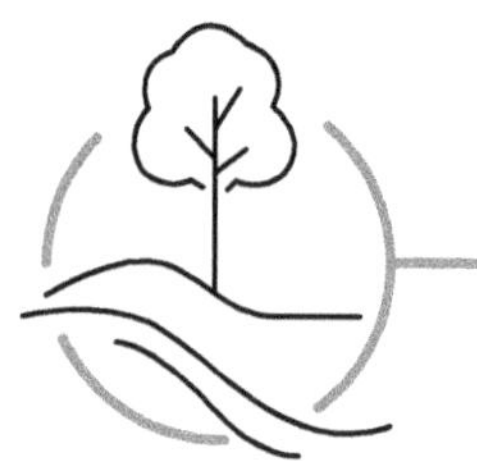

Habitat

Southern Cassowaries are found in tropical rainforests and dense woodlands. They require dense vegetation and access to water sources, such as rivers or streams, to survive.

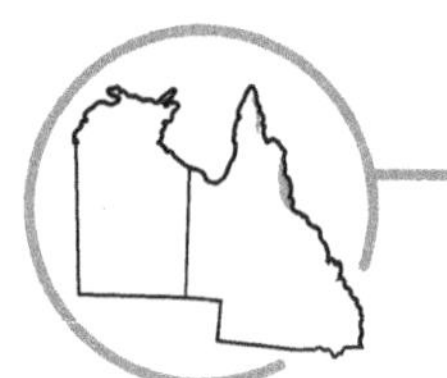

Distribution

Southern Cassowaries are found in the tropical rainforests of north-eastern Australia. Their range is limited to the Wet Tropics region of far north Queensland, including the Daintree Rainforest, Atherton Tableland, and surrounding areas.

Bird Journal

Date seen: Time seen:

Location:

Observations:

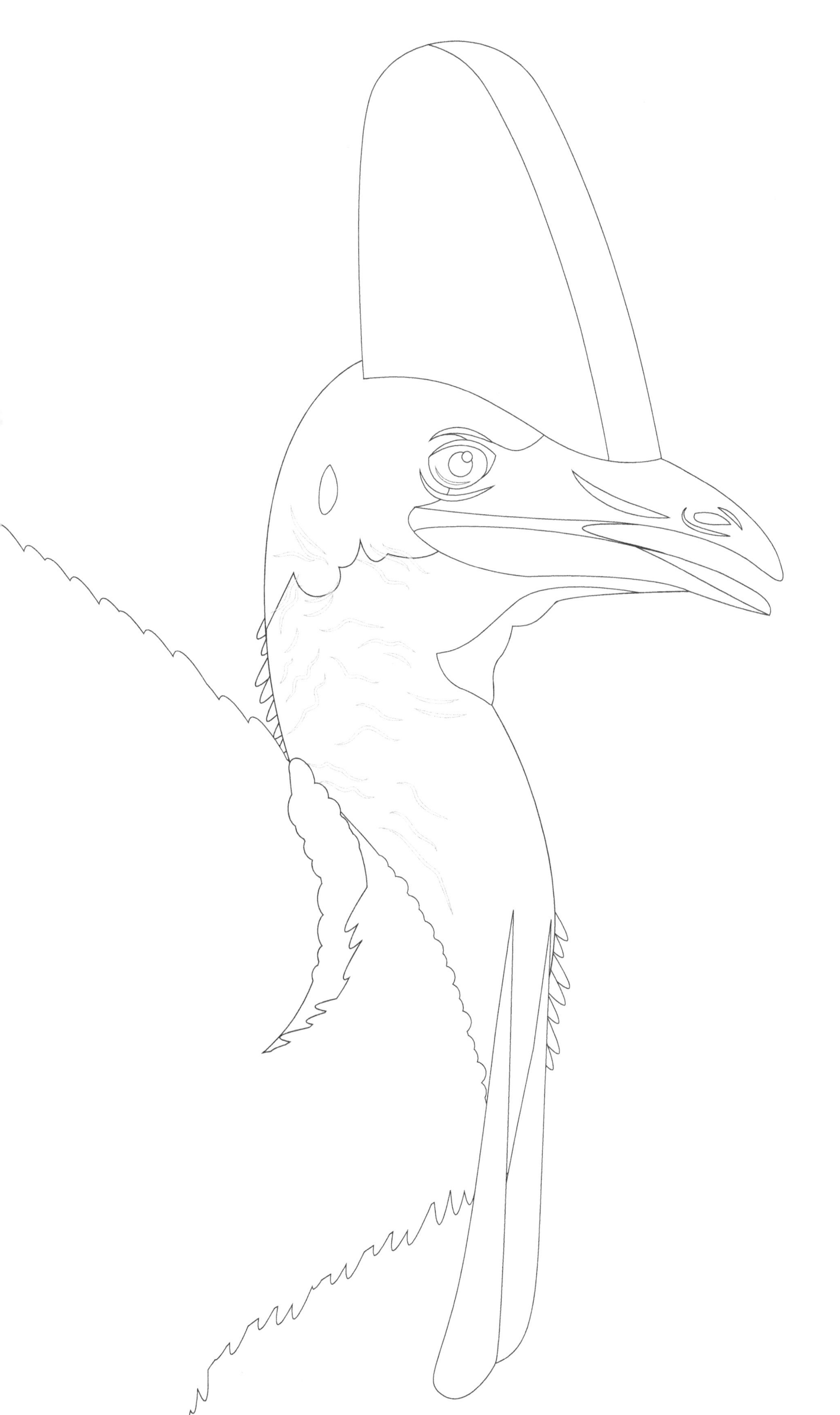

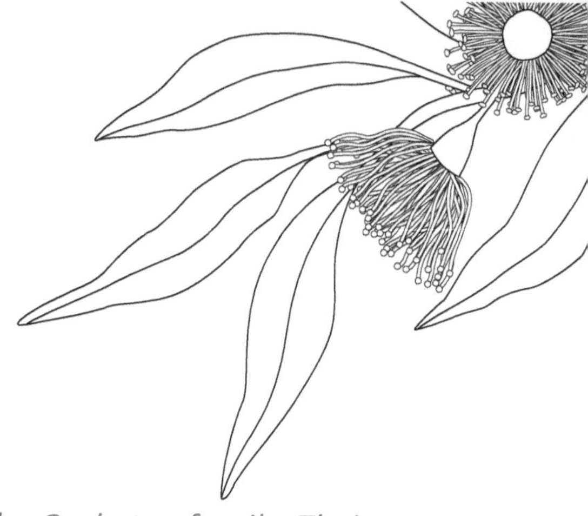

Cockatiel

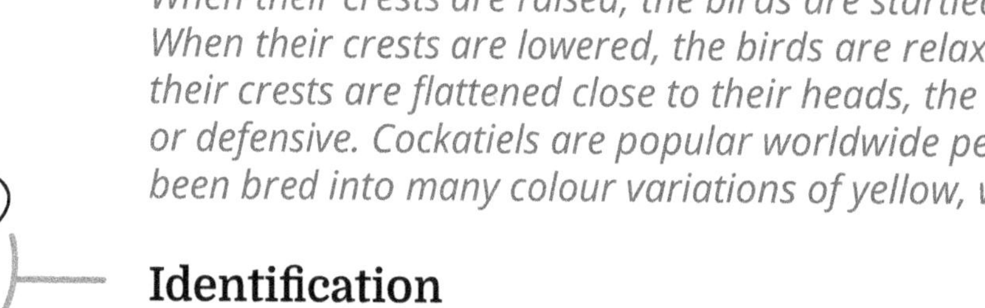

Cockatiels are the smallest species in the Cockatoo family. Their crest feathers change direction depending on their emotions. When their crests are raised, the birds are startled or excited. When their crests are lowered, the birds are relaxed and when their crests are flattened close to their heads, the birds are angry or defensive. Cockatiels are popular worldwide pets that have been bred into many colour variations of yellow, white and grey.

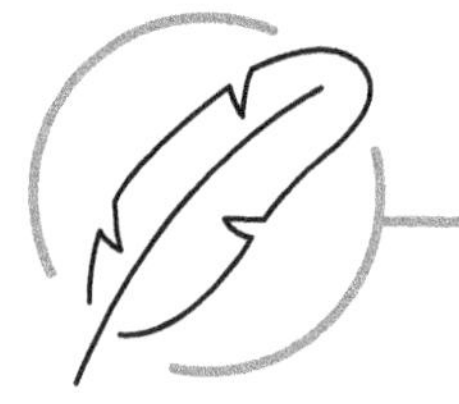

Identification

Cockatiels are identified by their unique fan-shaped crests. Cockatiels in the wild are grey, with white strips on the outer edges of their wings. Male faces are bright yellow or white, while female faces are grey or light grey. Both males and females have round orange patches on both cheeks. The male's cheeks are brighter than the female's. Their crest feathers are yellow and grey.

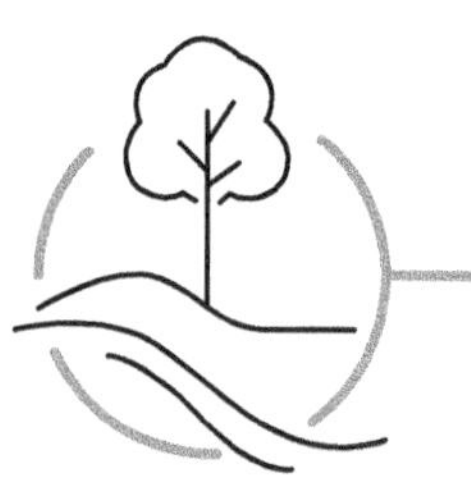

Habitat

Cockatiels are adaptable and can be found in habitats including open woodlands, scrublands, and grasslands. They are often seen in pairs or smaller flocks. Sometimes, hundreds will flock around a single body of water.

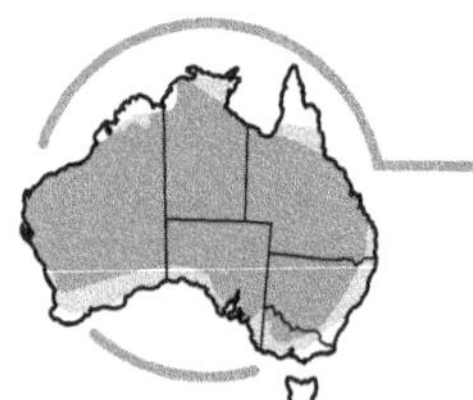

Distribution

Cockatiels are widespread throughout the mainland of Australia, except for the far north and south-east coastal regions. They are most commonly found in the semi-arid regions, including the inland areas of Queensland, New South Wales, and Victoria.

Bird Journal

Date seen:

Time seen:

Location:

Observations:

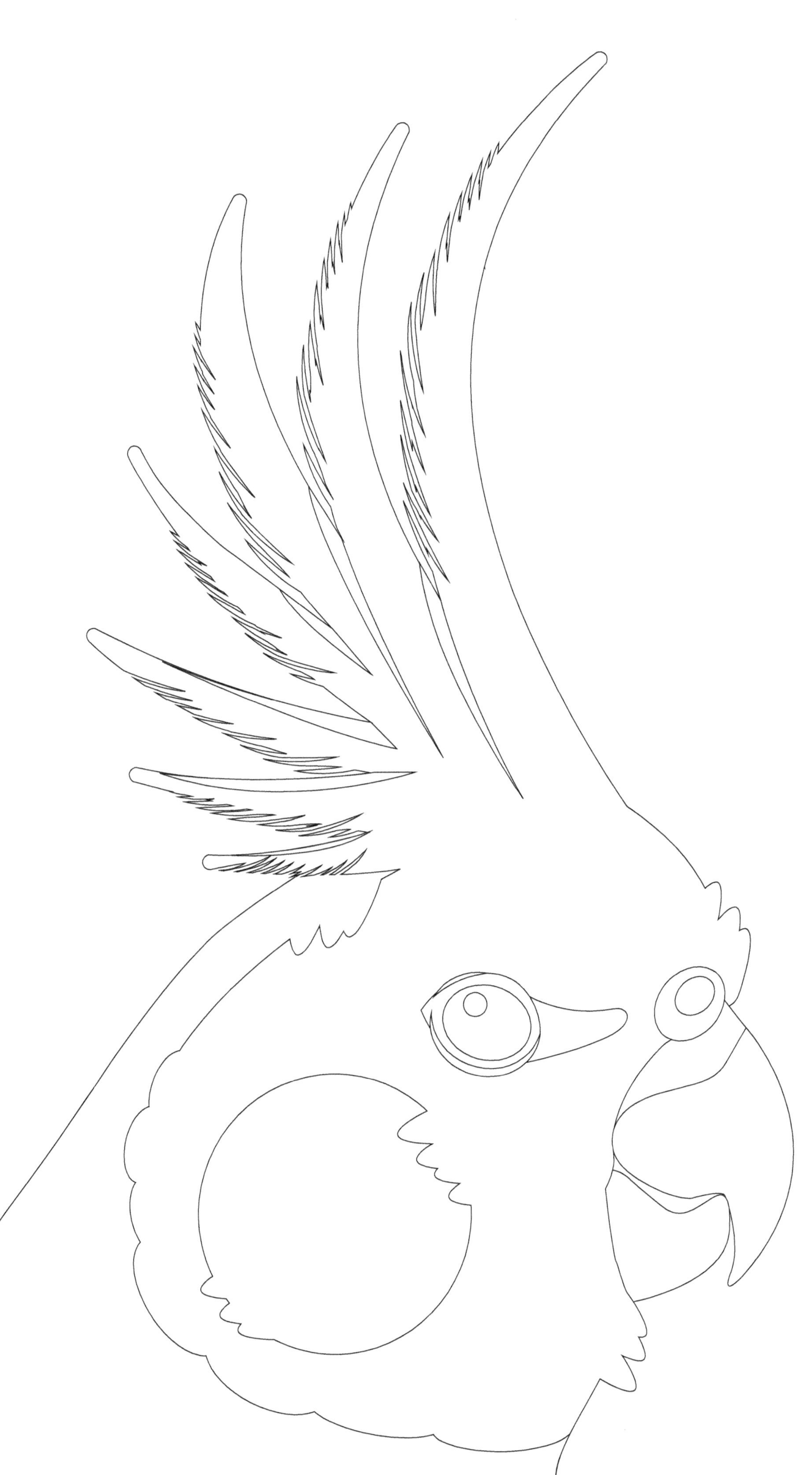

Gang-gang

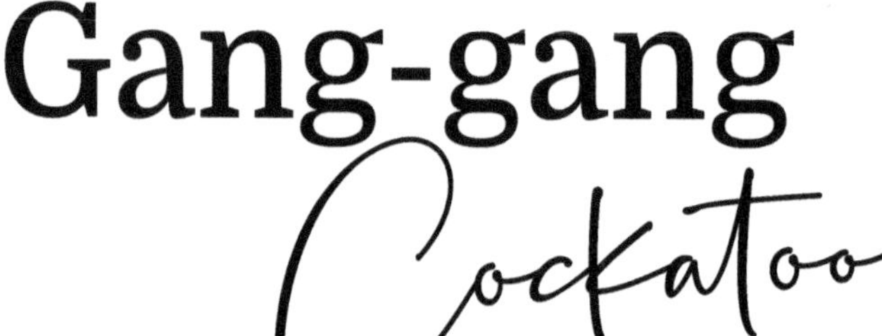

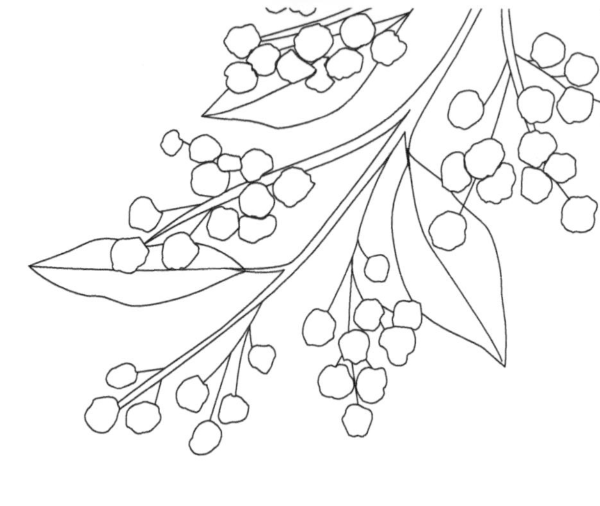

Gang-gang Cockatoos have a unique call that sounds like a creaky gate or a rusty hinge. They are usually heard before they are seen. Despite their name, they are not social birds and are seen in pairs or small groups.

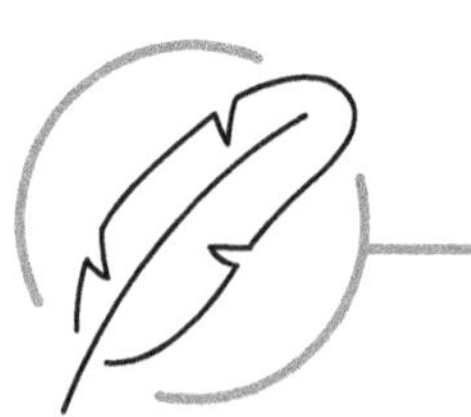

Identification

Gang-gang Cockatoos are small, dark grey cockatoos, with wispy crests that curl forward and short square tails. The males' heads and crests are bright red and the feathers on their bodies and wings are edged with light grey. Females' heads and crests are grey, with feathers edged with yellow and pink on their breasts and bellies, giving a barred appearance.

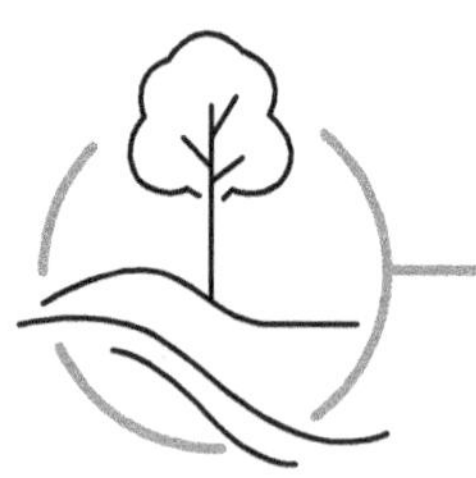

Habitat

Gang-gang Cockatoos are found in a range of forest types, including wet and dry Eucalypt woodlands in the mountains with dense shrub, as well as tall open forests. These birds migrate with the changing seasons, moving to more open habitats during autumn and winter, before returning to denser forests during breeding season. They require tall trees to build their nests.

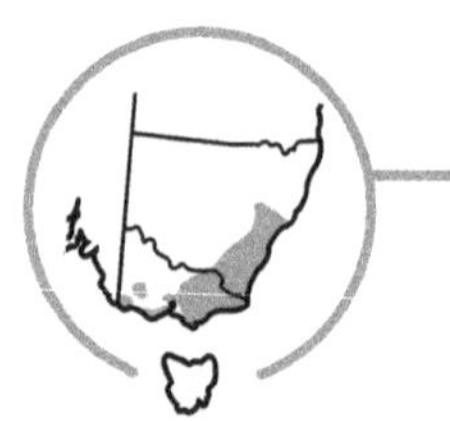

Distribution

Gang-gang Cockatoos are found in coastal regions of south-east Australia. From eastern New South Wales, the Hunter region, Central Tablelands and south-western Slopes, to southern Victoria, Gippsland region & Central Highlands.

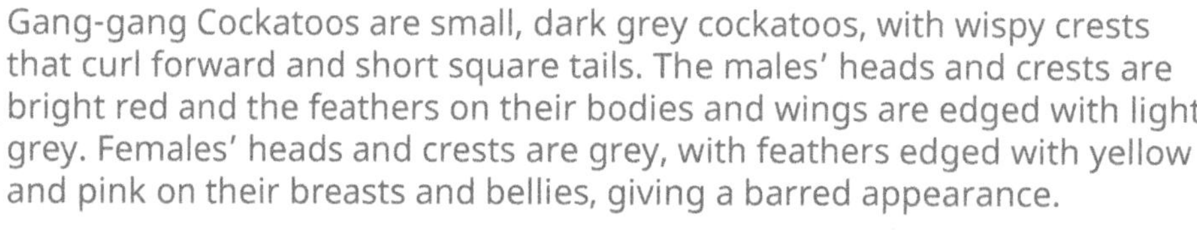

Bird Journal

Date seen: _______________________   Time seen: _______________________

Location: _______________________

Observations: _______________________

____

____

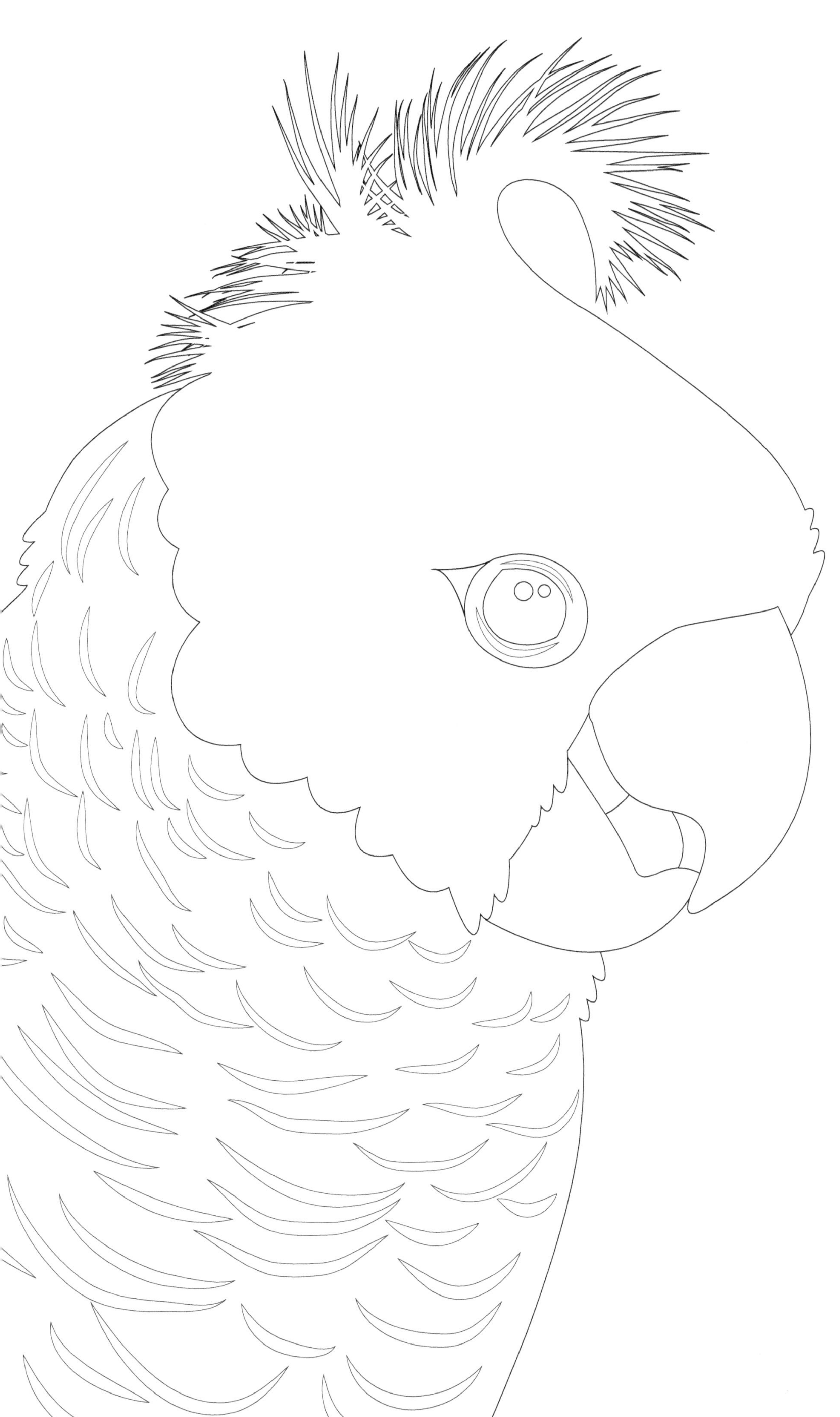

Major Mitchell's Cockatoo

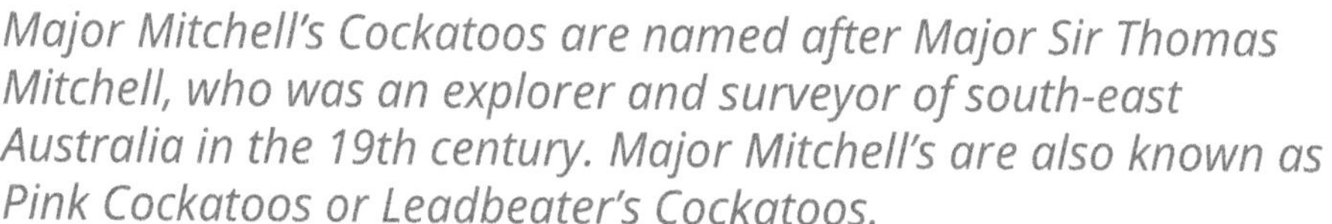

Major Mitchell's Cockatoos are named after Major Sir Thomas Mitchell, who was an explorer and surveyor of south-east Australia in the 19th century. Major Mitchell's are also known as Pink Cockatoos or Leadbeater's Cockatoos.

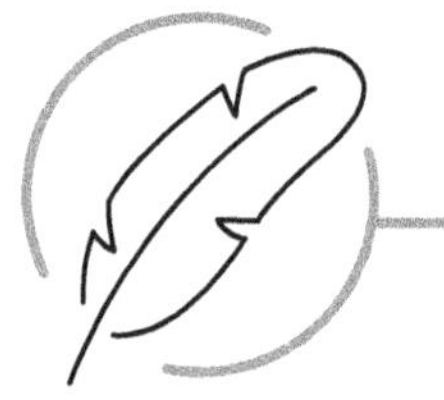

Identification

Major Mitchell's are known for being one of the most beautiful cockatoos. They have soft white feathers on their backs and pale pink feathers on their breasts and bellies. They have long, forward pointing bright red and yellow banded crests. Wings and flight feathers are white, with their underwings bright orange-pink. Males and females are almost identical in appearance. Males are slightly larger and have dark brown eyes, while females have pink or red eyes.

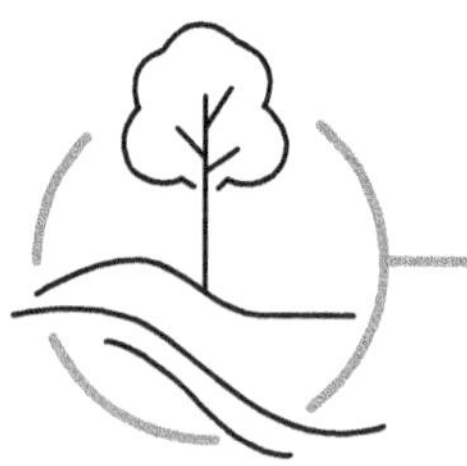

Habitat

Major Mitchell's are often found in open woodland areas, as well as in shrublands and grasslands. They need forested areas for nesting and prefer habitats near a reliable source of water, such as rivers and waterholes.

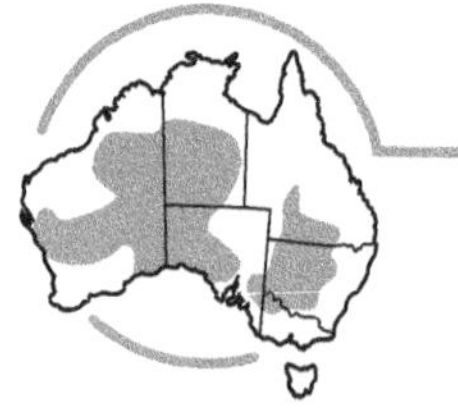

Distribution

Major Mitchell's inhabit Australia's semi-arid and arid inland areas. They can be found in south Queensland, north-western Victoria, South Australia, south-western Northern Territory, and along the west coast from Shark Bay to Jurien. In New South Wales, these cockatoos are a common sight in the areas of Bourke and Griffith.

Bird Journal

Date seen: Time seen:

Location:

Observations:

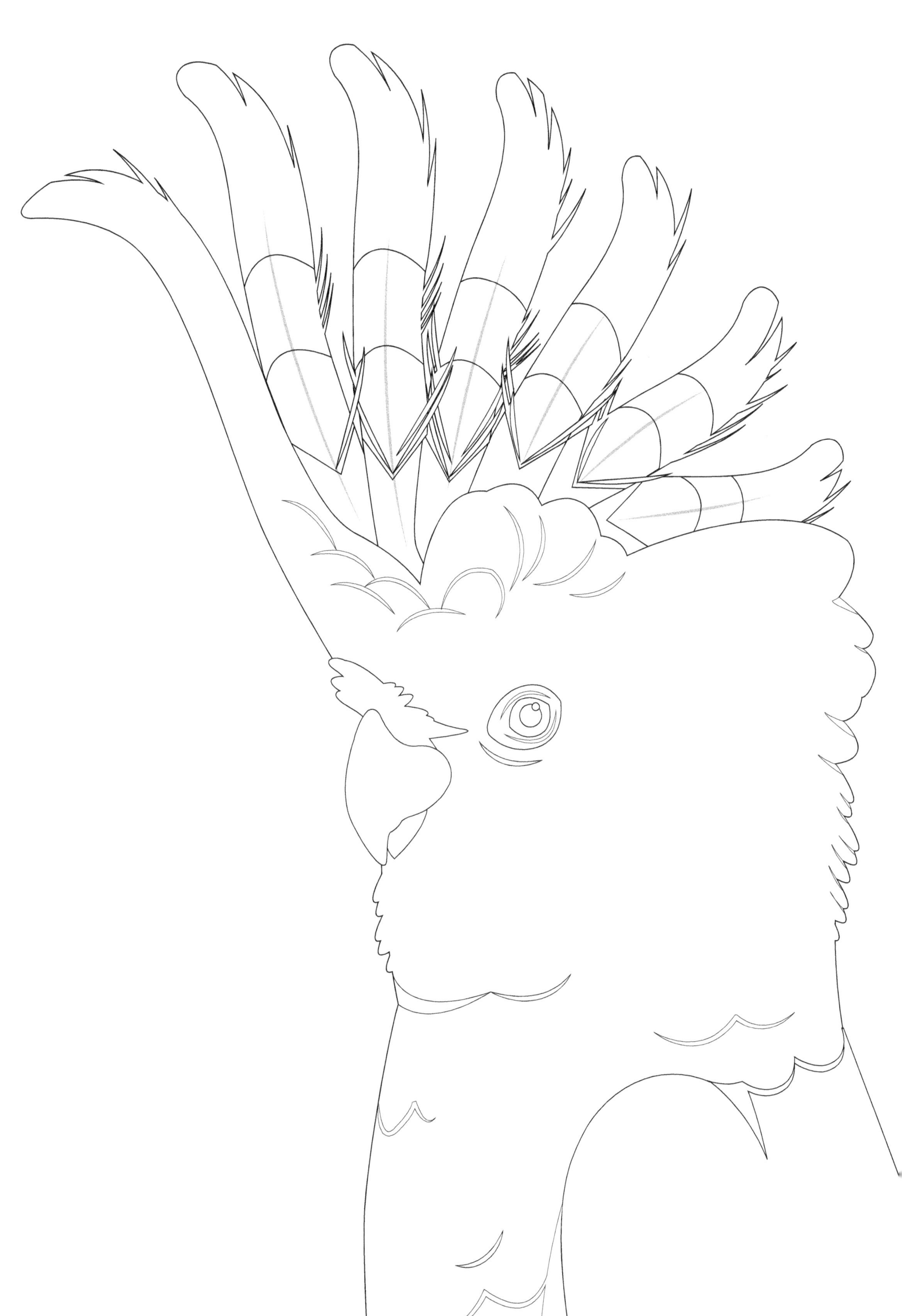

Red-tailed *Black-Cockatoo*

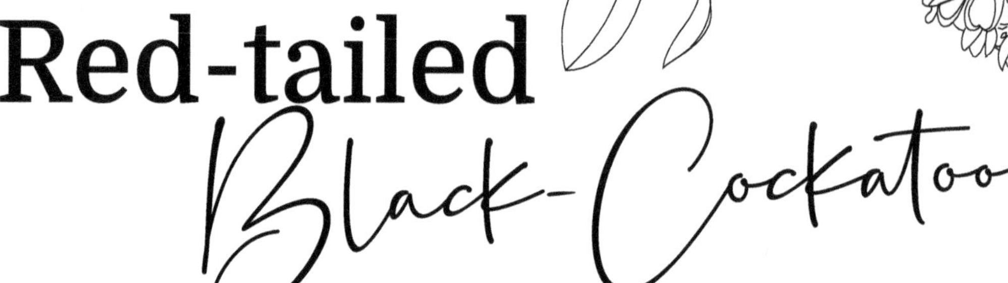

Red-tailed Black-Cockatoos have a loud and distinctive call, a series of high-pitched screeches. They are often seen in small groups or pairs, and fly in a slow, wavy pattern. There are five subspecies of Red-tailed Black-Cockatoos in Australia, all with different sized beaks.

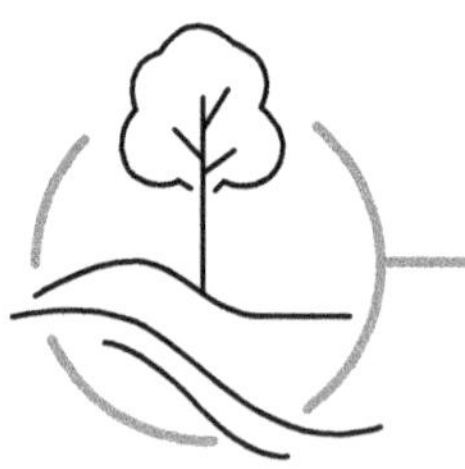

Identification

Red-tailed Black-Cockatoos have distinctive black feathers with raised crest feathers. However, males and females look quite different. The males are glossy black with bright red panels on their tail feathers. The females have duller black feathers with yellow-orange stripes on their chests and yellow spots on their cheeks, neck and wings. Their tail feathers also feature yellow-orange stripes.

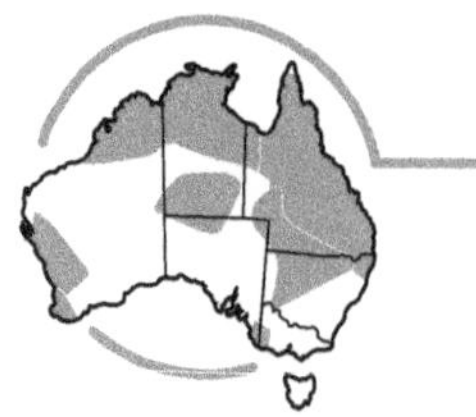

Habitat

Red-tailed Black-Cockatoos are found in a range of habitats, including Eucalyptus forests or woodlands (especially if they have experienced fire), tropical savannahs and desert rangelands. They depend on large, old Eucalyptus trees for nesting hollows.

Distribution

Red-tailed Black-Cockatoos are found across drier parts of Australia, ranging across northern and eastern Australia. Queensland, the Northern Territory, Western Victoria, New South Wales and the south-western corner of Western Australia all have different subspecies. Forest Red-tailed Black-Cockatoos in Western Australia are vulnerable and South-eastern Red-tailed Black-Cockatoos in Victoria are endangered.

Bird Journal

Date seen: ___________________   Time seen: ___________________

Location: ___________________

Observations: ___________________
____
____

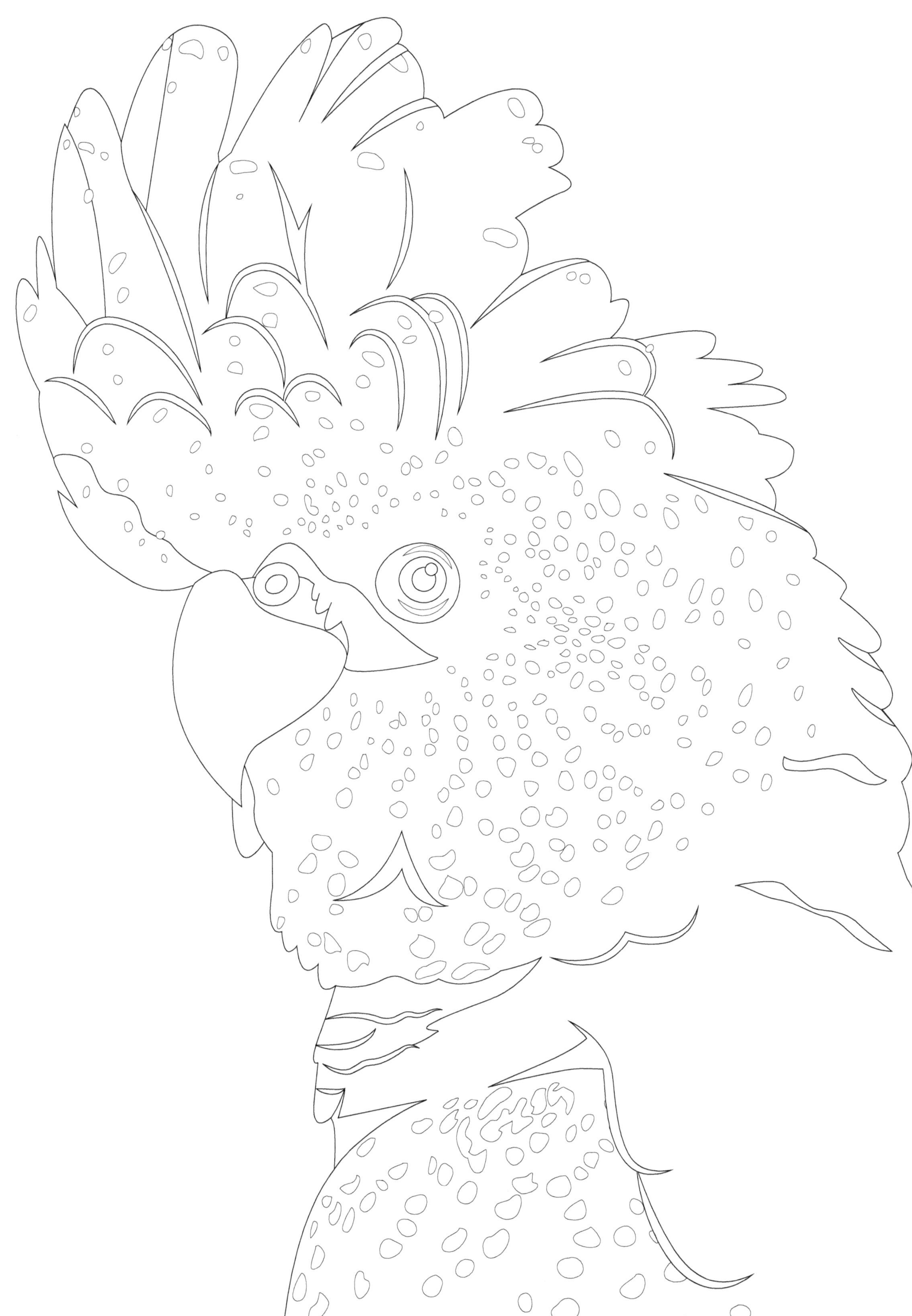

Sulphur-crested
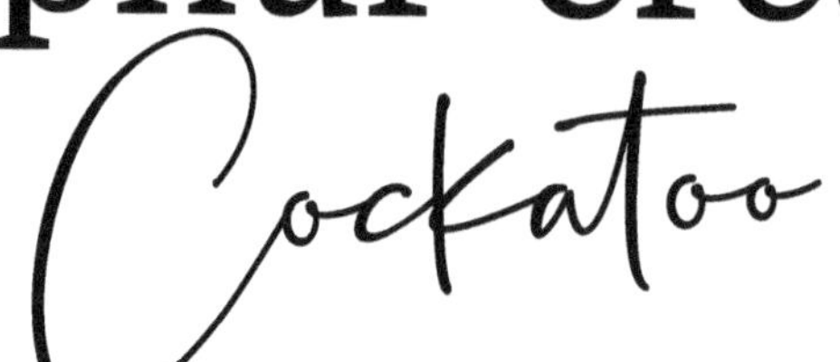

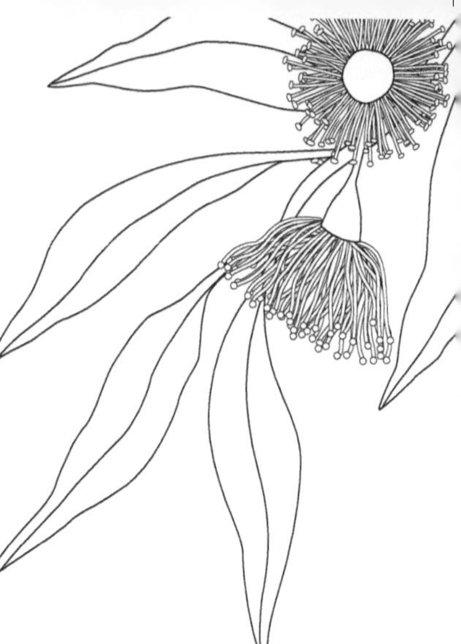

Sulphur-crested Cockatoos produce a very fine powder that waterproofs their feathers instead of oil, which many other birds use. The powder is made from keratin, the same material that makes up human hair and nails.

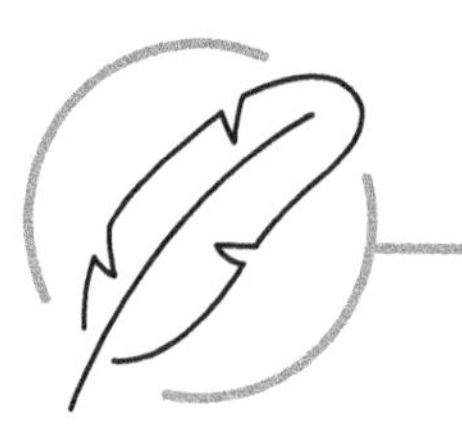

Identification

Sulphur-crested Cockatoos are large white parrots that are very noisy. They have a distinctive yellow crests and their underwings, cheeks and tails have a pale yellow tinge. They have powerful beaks that are adapted to cracking open nuts and seeds. Males and females are similar in appearance, the only difference being eye colour. Males have almost black eyes and females have red or brown eyes.

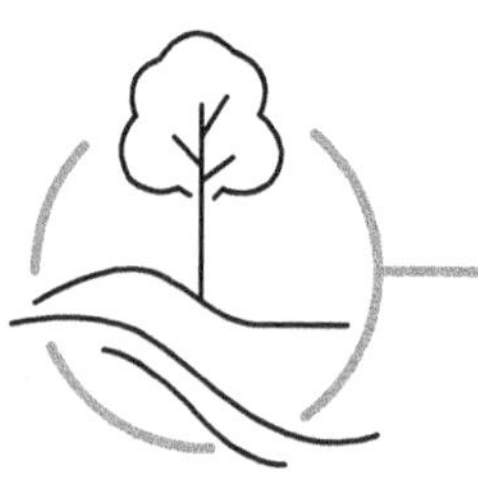

Habitat

Sulphur-crested Cockatoos are found in a variety of habitats with trees close to water, such as tropical swamps and mangroves, woodlands, Eucalypt forests, and savannahs. They are adaptable birds and live in suburban and urban areas.

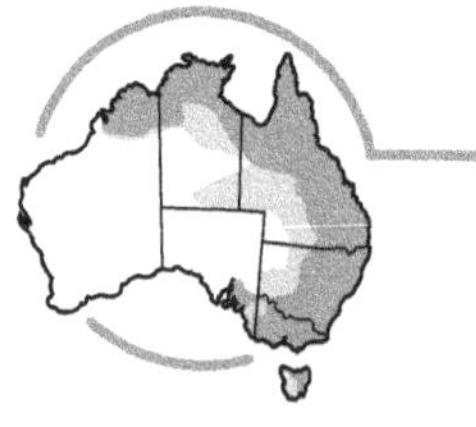

Distribution

Sulphur-crested Cockatoos can be found throughout northern and eastern Australia, as well as in Tasmania.

Date seen: **Time seen:**

Location:

Observations:

Bird Journal

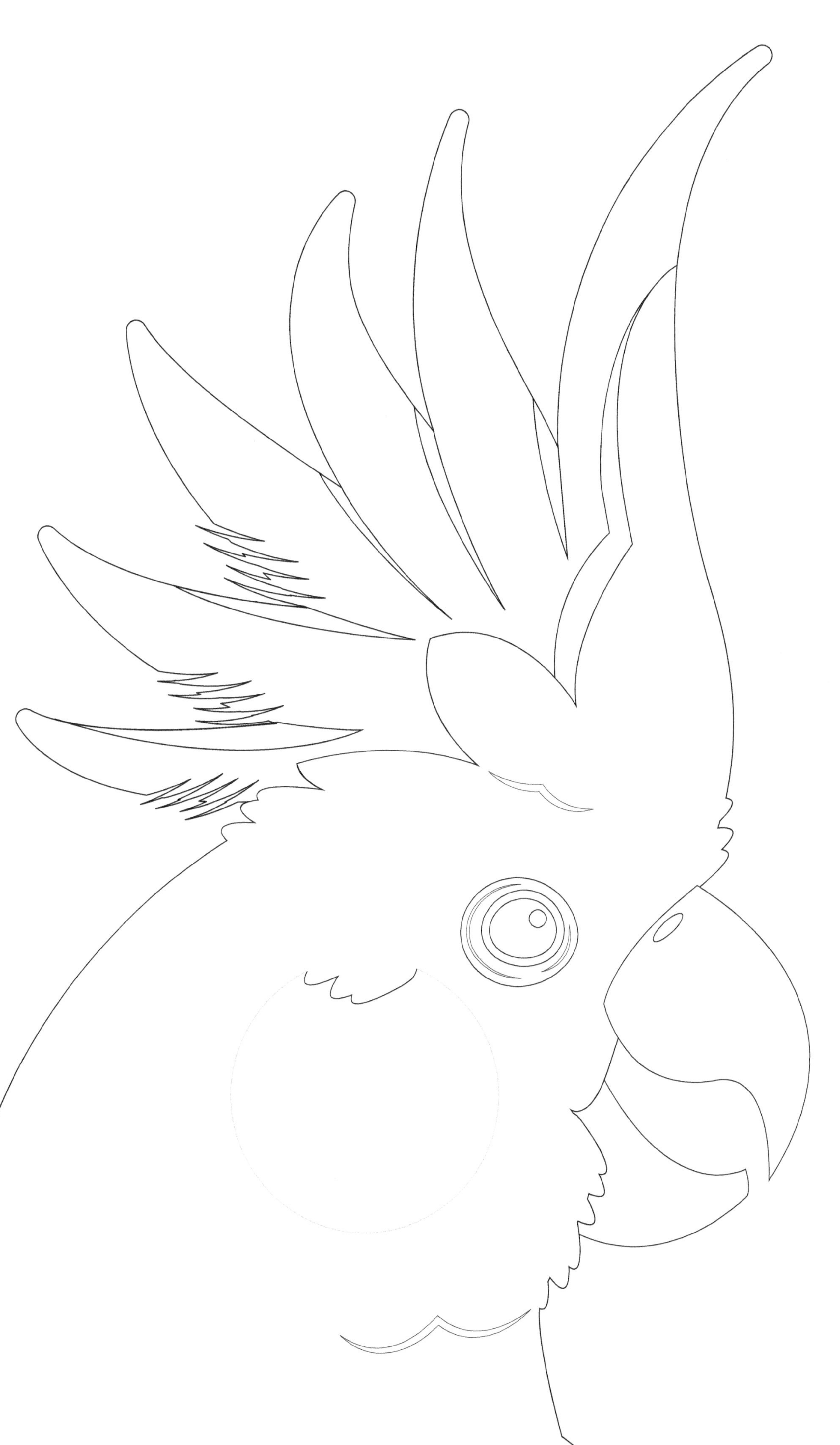

Australian 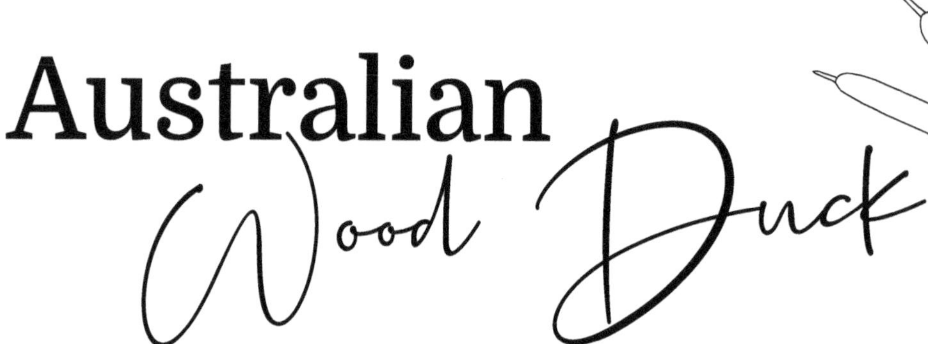 Wood Duck

Unlike most ducks, Australian Wood Ducks spend much of their life with one mate. Both parents take part in raising the young, the male taking on most of the responsibility for guarding the nest and the female leading the ducklings to water.

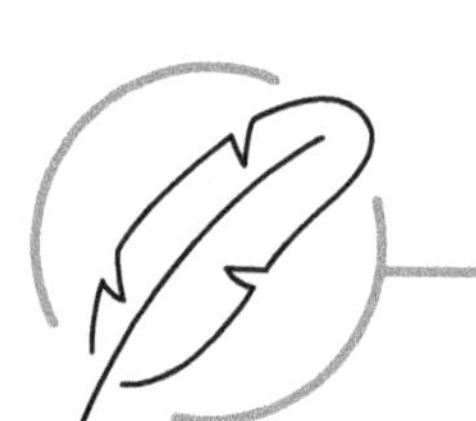

Identification

Australian Wood Ducks are medium-sized ducks with dark brown heads and pale bodies with two black stripes along their backs. Male Wood Ducks have small manes and brown-grey chests that are speckled, while their lower bellies and under-tails are black. Female Wood Ducks have lighter brown heads with white stripes above and below their eyes, and their chests and wings are speckled. Their lower bellies and under-tails are white. They can easily walk on land.

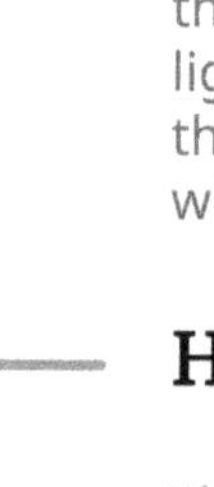

Habitat

The Australian Wood Duck is an adaptable species that is found in a range of habitats across Australia, such as freshwater wetlands including swamps, marshes and billabongs, and rivers and lakes. Australian Wood Ducks are also found in agricultural lands, such as paddocks and pastures, and in parks and gardens in urban areas.

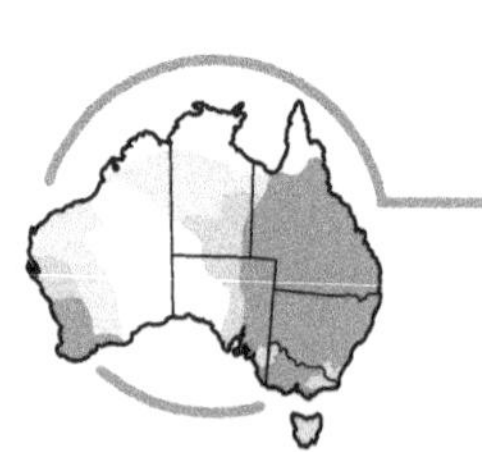

Distribution

Australian Wood Ducks are widespread in Australia. Their range extends from the tropical regions of northern Australia down to Tasmania, and from the eastern coast of Australia to the west coast.

Bird Journal

Date seen: Time seen:

Location:

Observations:

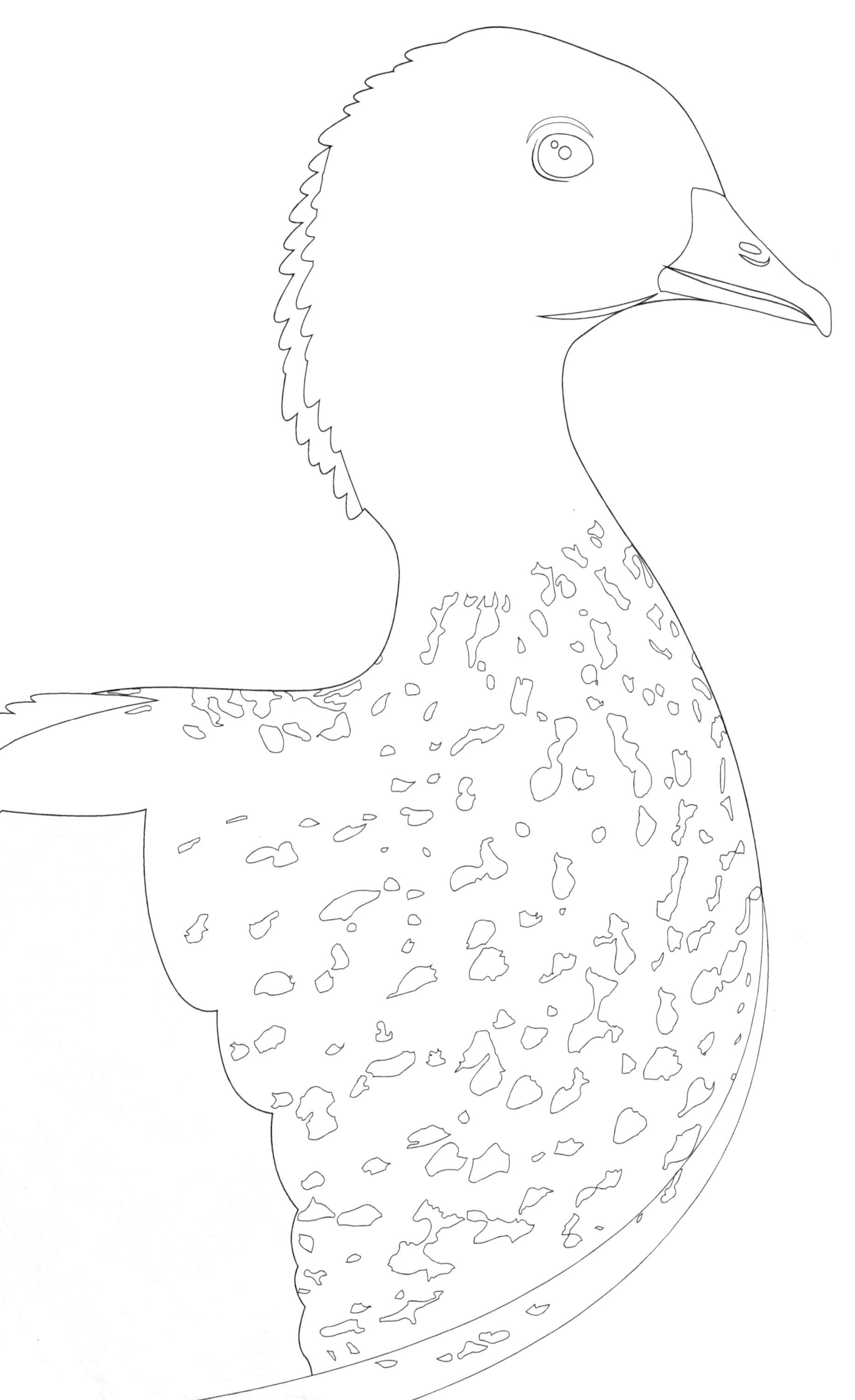

Emu

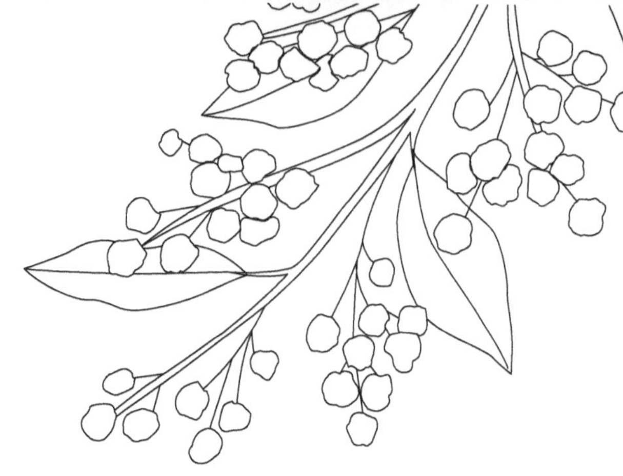

Emus produce a variety of sounds, including booms, drumming, and grunts. The booming sounds are made by the Emu's inflatable neck sac and can be heard from distances up to two kilometres.

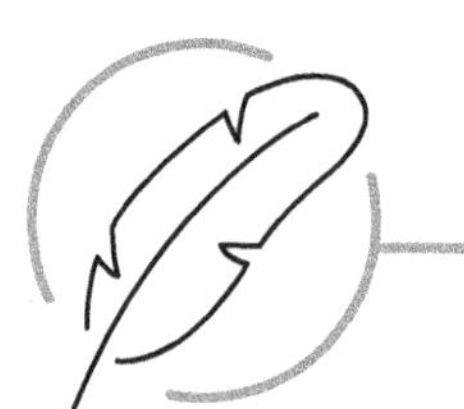

Identification

Emus are Australia's tallest native birds. They can grow up to 1.9 metres tall. Emus have a unique appearance with long necks, slender legs and small heads with pointed, curved beaks. They are covered in shaggy grey-brown feathers, except for their necks and heads, which are covered in blue-grey skin. Although Emus have small wings that prevent them from flying, they make up for it with their powerful legs. Each leg has three toes with sharp claws that are used for defence and for digging.

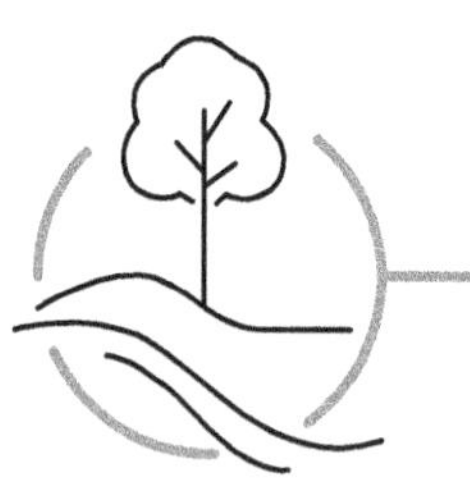

Habitat

Emus are found in a range of habitats, including forests, grasslands, savannahs, and scrublands. Emus prefer areas with open spaces that allow them to move around. They are adaptable birds and can survive in a range of climates, from deserts to snowy regions. Emus are also known to move into urban areas if there are reliable sources of food and water available.

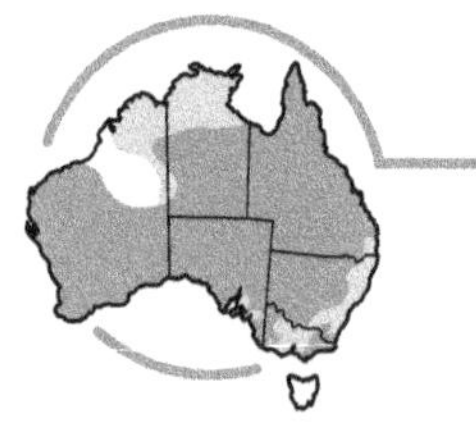

Distribution

Emus live throughout most of Australia, ranging from coastal areas to the Snowy Mountains. They are most commonly found in the drier, more remote areas of the country. Some states with significant Emu populations include Western Australia, South Australia, and Queensland.

Bird Journal

Date seen: **Time seen:**

Location:

Observations:

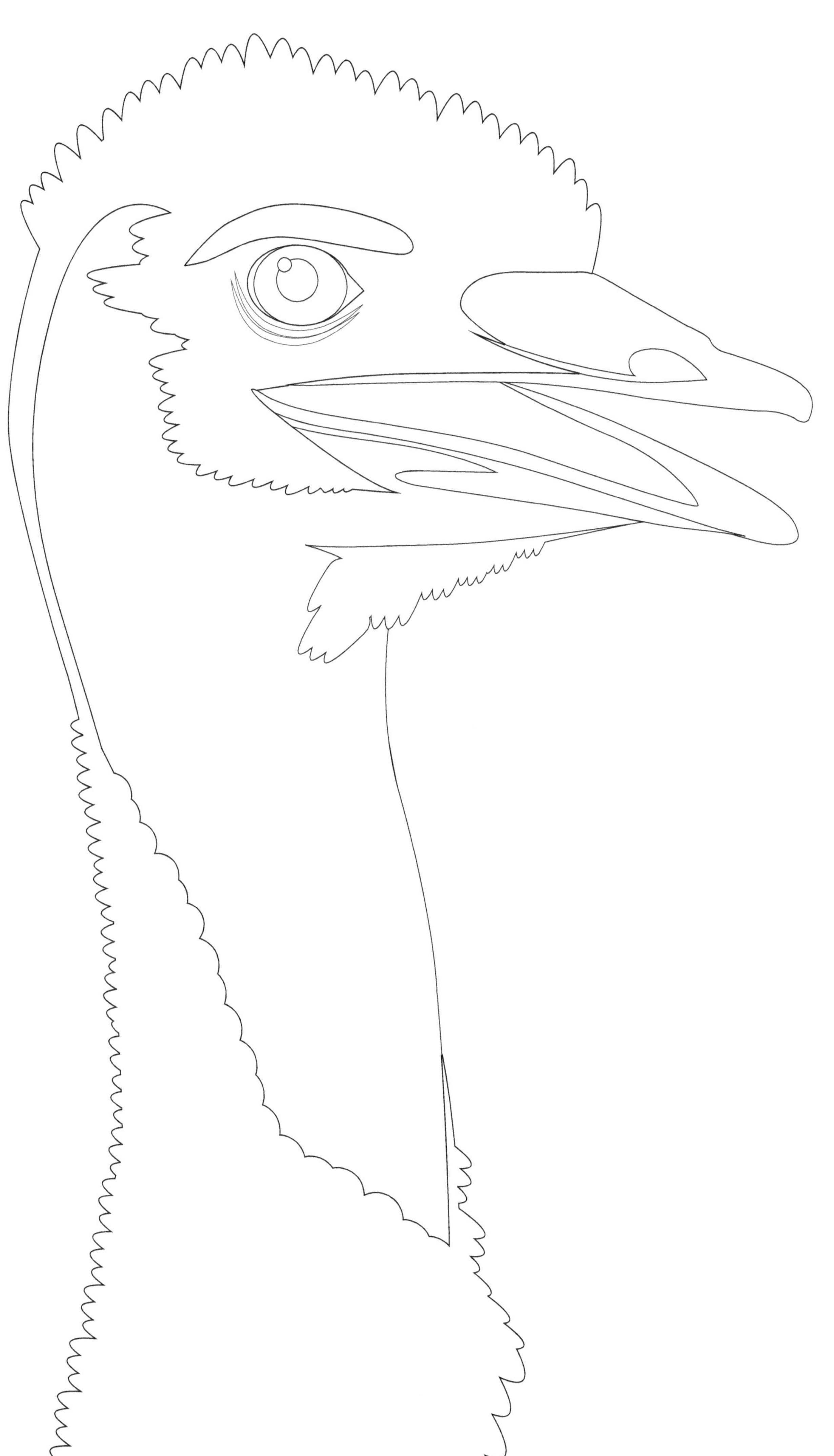

Superb Fairy-wren

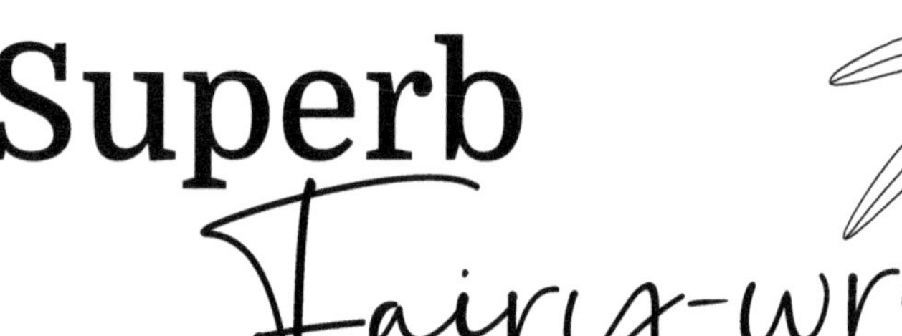

The male Superb Fairy-wren's feathers change colour during mating season, from dull brown to bright blue. Bright colours help attract a mate, but this also makes it difficult to hide from predators.

Identification

Superb Fairy-wren males are brightly coloured, with light blue crowns and cheeks, a black band surrounding their eyes, and dark blue throats. Their wings are brown, while their chests and bellies are white. Their beaks are black and they have brown legs. Males will fan out their blue tail feathers to impress females. Female Superb Fairy-wrens have brown feathers with white throats, chests and bellies, and they have orange-red beaks and eye bands. Their tails are brown with a pale blue-grey tinge.

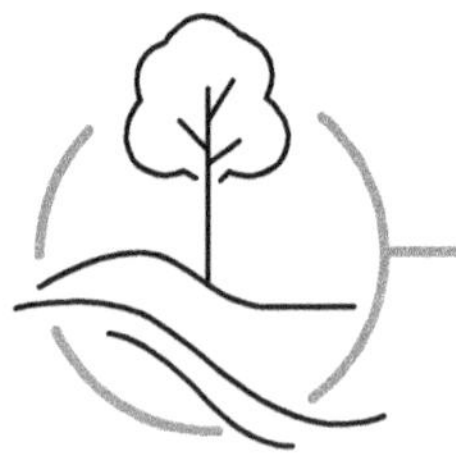

Habitat

Superb Fairy-wrens are found in a range of habitats, including open woodlands, scrublands, and forests with dense undergrowth. They are also known to inhabit urban areas with vegetation cover such as parks and gardens. They can be found in weeds such as lantana and are seen in pairs or small groups.

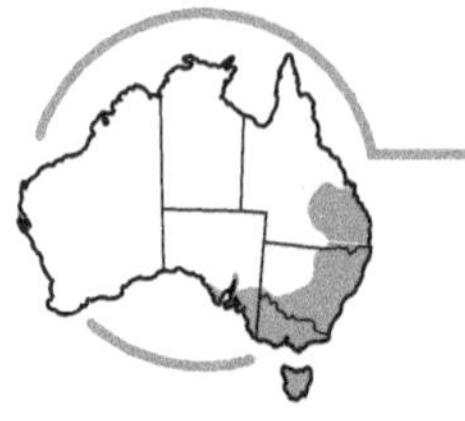

Distribution

The distribution of Superb Fairy-wrens spans across south-eastern Australia, including regions from south-eastern Queensland and eastern New South Wales, through to southern Eyre Peninsula in South Australia and Tasmania.

Bird Journal

Date seen: Time seen:

Location:

Observations:

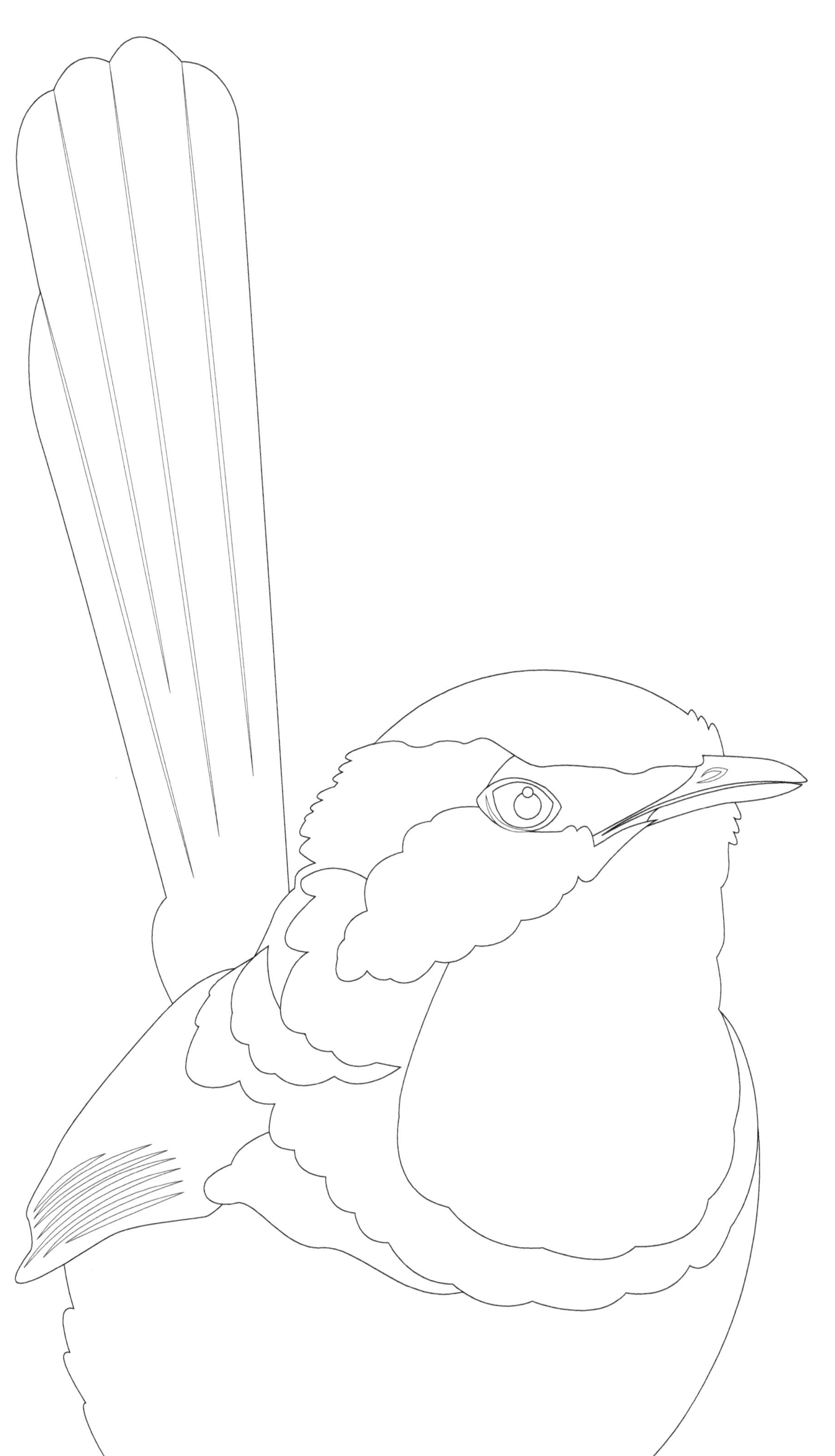

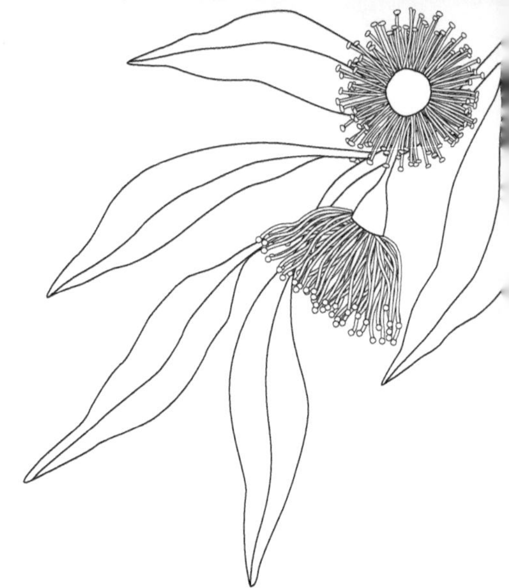

Gouldian
Finch

Gouldian Finches have unique beaks, which are curved and adapted for cracking open grass seeds. Gouldian finches will eat up to 35% of their body weight in seeds every day.

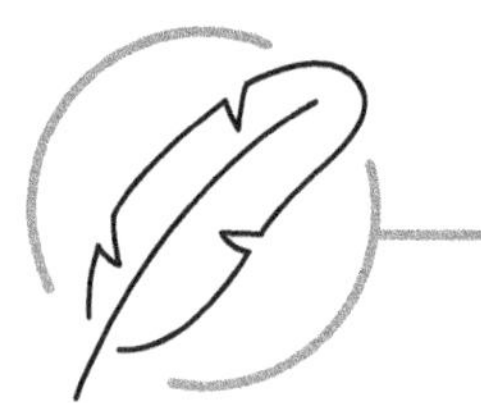

Identification

Gouldian Finches are known for their coloured feathers. These small birds have purple chests, bright green backs and yellow bellies, with a blue ring around their faces. Gouldian Finches can have one of three face colours. 75% can black faces, while 25% have red faces. A rare yellow-faced Finch might appear because of a lack of red pigment in red-faced birds.

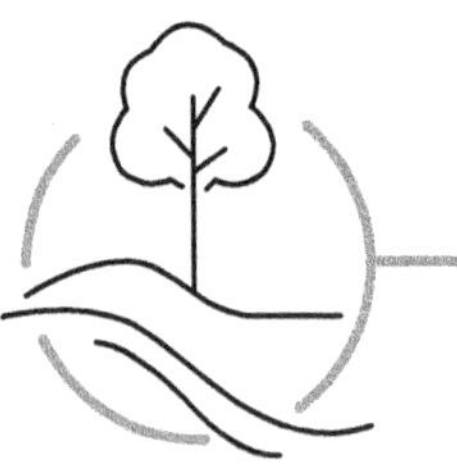

Habitat

Gouldian Finches can be found in open, grassy Eucalypt woodlands and grasslands of tropics. They stay close to water, such as rivers and creeks, and must drink frequently throughout the day.

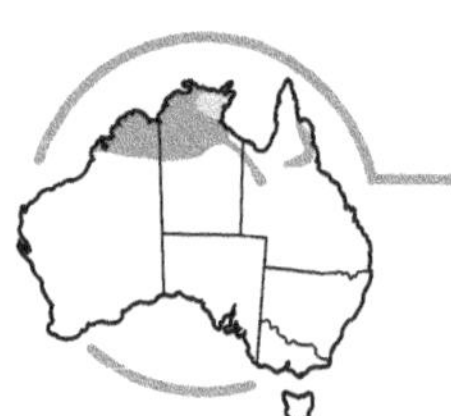

Distribution

Gouldian Finches can be found in the northern parts of Australia, specifically the Kimberley region of Western Australia, the Top End of the Northern Territory, and in parts of Queensland.

Bird Journal

Date seen: _______________________   Time seen: _______________________

Location: ____

Observations: ____

____

____

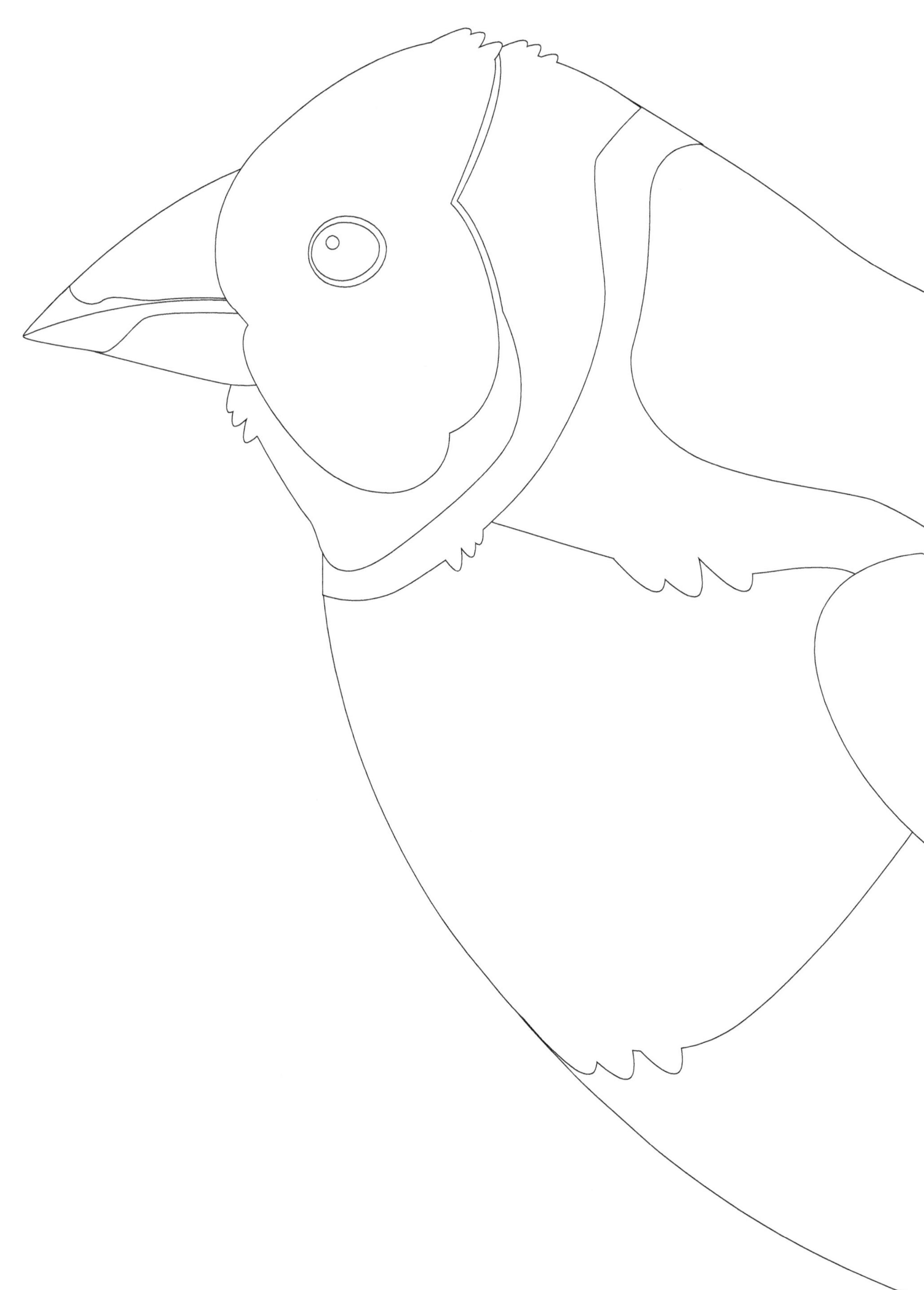

Galah

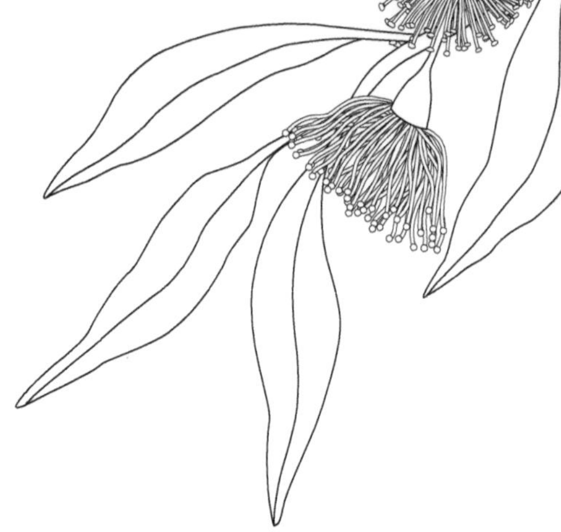

Galahs are cavity nesters, and they require nesting sites in trees or other vegetation. They often nest in dead or dying trees. Galahs are also known to strip bark from trees near their nest sites to create a larger entrance hole and to collect nesting material.

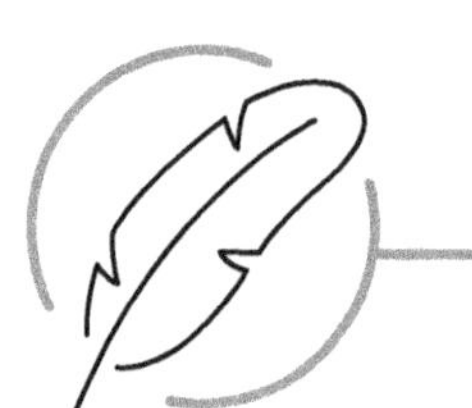

Identification

Galahs are medium-sized cockatoos with unique pink and grey feathers. Their heads, necks, and underbellies are pink and their crests are lighter pink. They have grey wings and tail feathers. Male and female Galahs look very similar, the only difference being eye colour. Males have dark brown eyes, while females have pinkish eyes. Galahs are often seen in flocks and are known for their distinctive screeching call, which can often be heard when they are in flight or perched in trees.

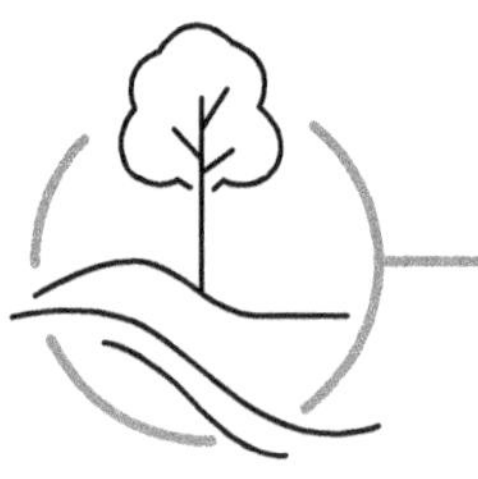

Habitat

Galahs are adaptable birds that are found in a range of habitats, including woodlands, savannahs, scrublands, and urban areas. In urban areas, they are often seen in parks and gardens. Galahs prefer open habitats with access to water and food sources.

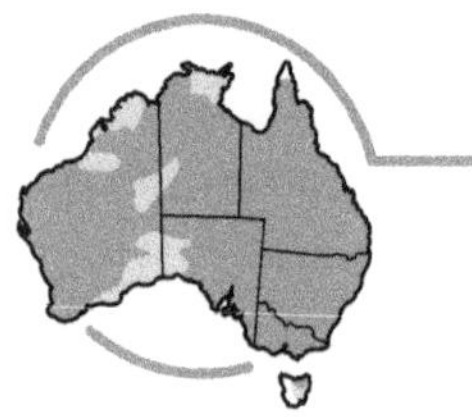

Distribution

Galahs are one of Australia's most common cockatoos. Galahs are found throughout most of Australia, except for the tropical northern regions and some parts of the arid interior.

Bird Journal

Date seen: _______________   Time seen: _______________

Location: _______________

Observations: _______________

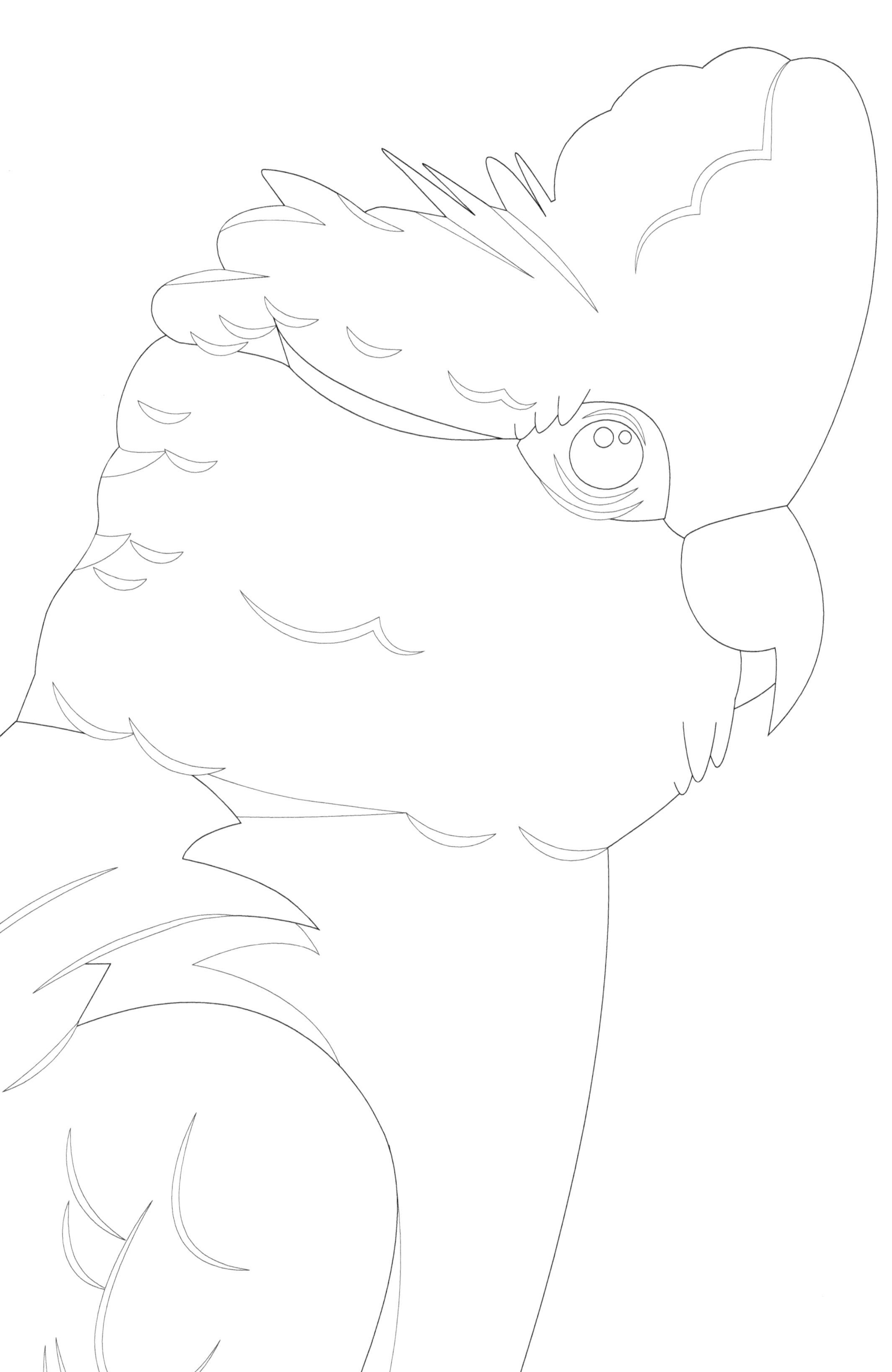

Australian King-Parrot

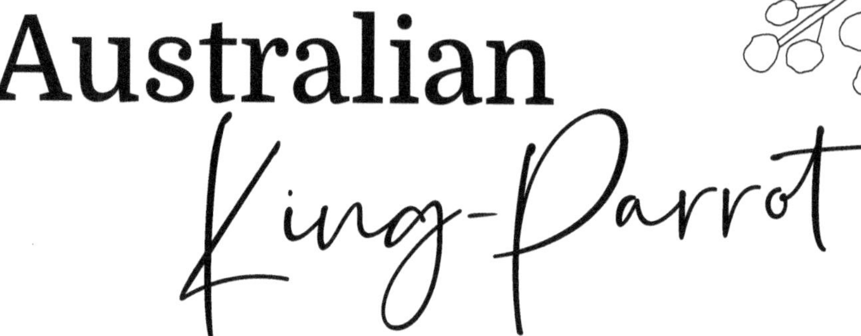

King-Parrots look red and green to humans. When viewed under ultraviolet light, the feathers on their wings have a yellow glow. Birds have four types of cones in their eyes, which is one more than humans, and this allows them to see into the ultraviolet part of the light spectrum.

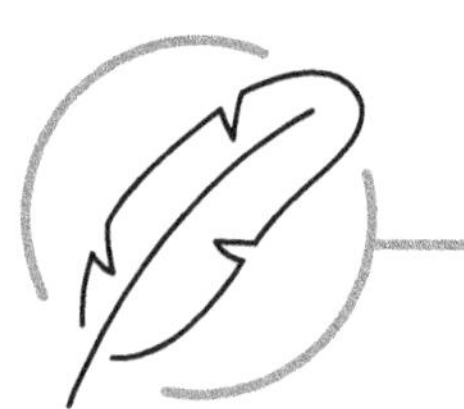

Identification

Australian King-Parrot males and females are quite different. The Male King-Parrots have bright red heads, necks and underparts, and bright green backs and wings. The females have green heads, necks and underparts, with light green bellies and breasts, and green backs and wings. Both males and females have bluish-green tail feathers, and they have a small patch of blue on their wings.

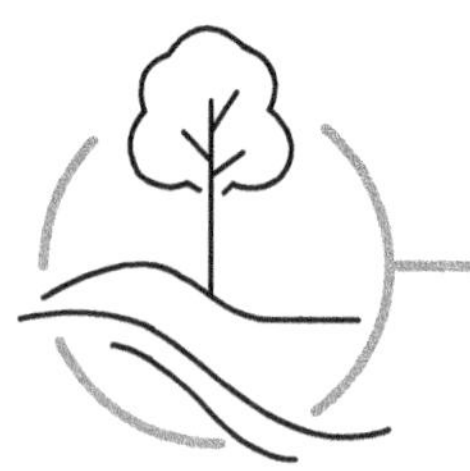

Habitat

King-Parrots are found in forested areas, including rainforests, Eucalypt forests, and woodlands. They prefer areas with a mix of tall trees and undergrowth, as well as clearings or forest edges. They are also known to inhabit gardens and parks in urban areas, particularly if these areas have tall trees or forested patches nearby.

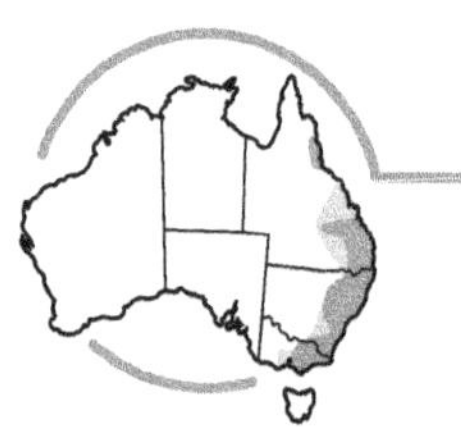

Distribution

King-Parrots are found in eastern and south-eastern Australia. Their distribution extends from far north Queensland down through eastern New South Wales, eastern Victoria and into south-eastern South Australia.

Bird Journal

Date seen: _______________________   Time seen: _______________________

Location: _______________________

Observations: _______________________

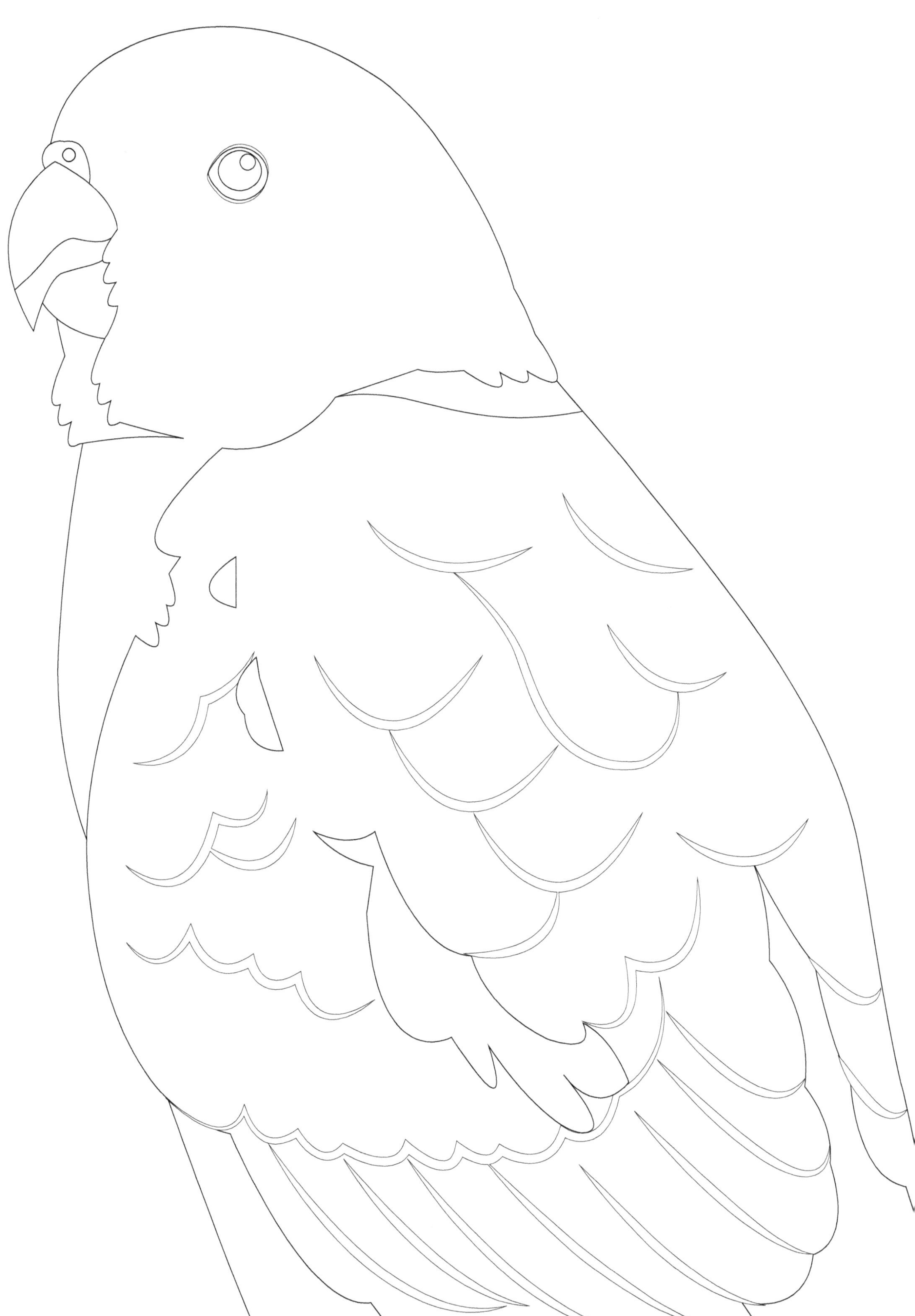

Azure
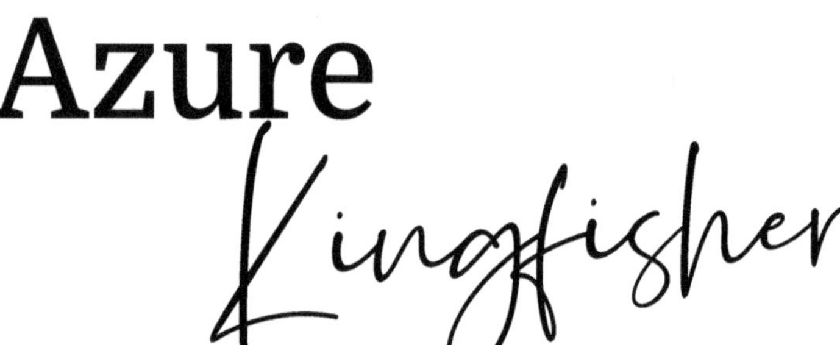
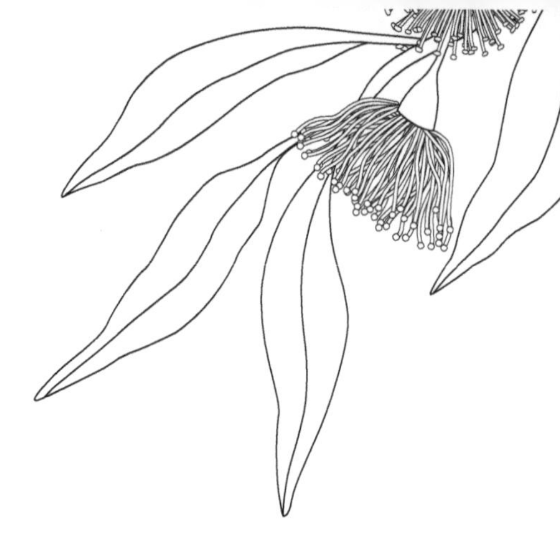

Azure Kingfishers have a unique hunting technique. They perch on low-hanging branches or vegetation, then plunge-dive headfirst into the water to catch their prey. They can do this with incredible accuracy, as they can adjust their eyes to see clearly both in air and water.

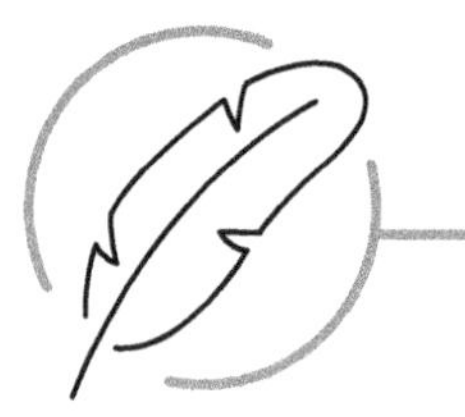

Identification

Azure Kingfishers are one of the smallest kingfisher species weighing only 25 - 40 grams. Azure Kingfishers have short tails and long, thin black beaks. Their heads, necks, backs and wings are a deep azure blue with a purple shine. They have a white stripe on each side of their necks and a small orange spot in front of each eye. Their throats are a pale orange-white colour that changes to a deeper orange colour on their bellies and under-tails. Their legs and feet are red.

Habitat

Azure Kingfishers are found in a range of freshwater habitats, including rivers, streams, creeks, billabongs, lakes, swamps and dams. They prefer shaded areas with overhanging vegetation or other perching spots, such as logs or rocks.

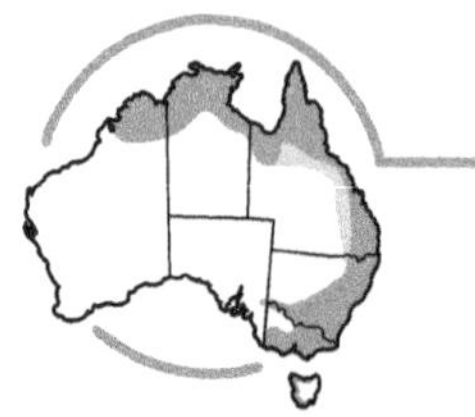

Distribution

Azure Kingfishers are found throughout much of northern and eastern Australia, including the coastal areas of Western Australia, Northern Territory, Queensland, New South Wales, Victoria and Tasmania.

Bird Journal

Date seen: **Time seen:**

Location:

Observations:

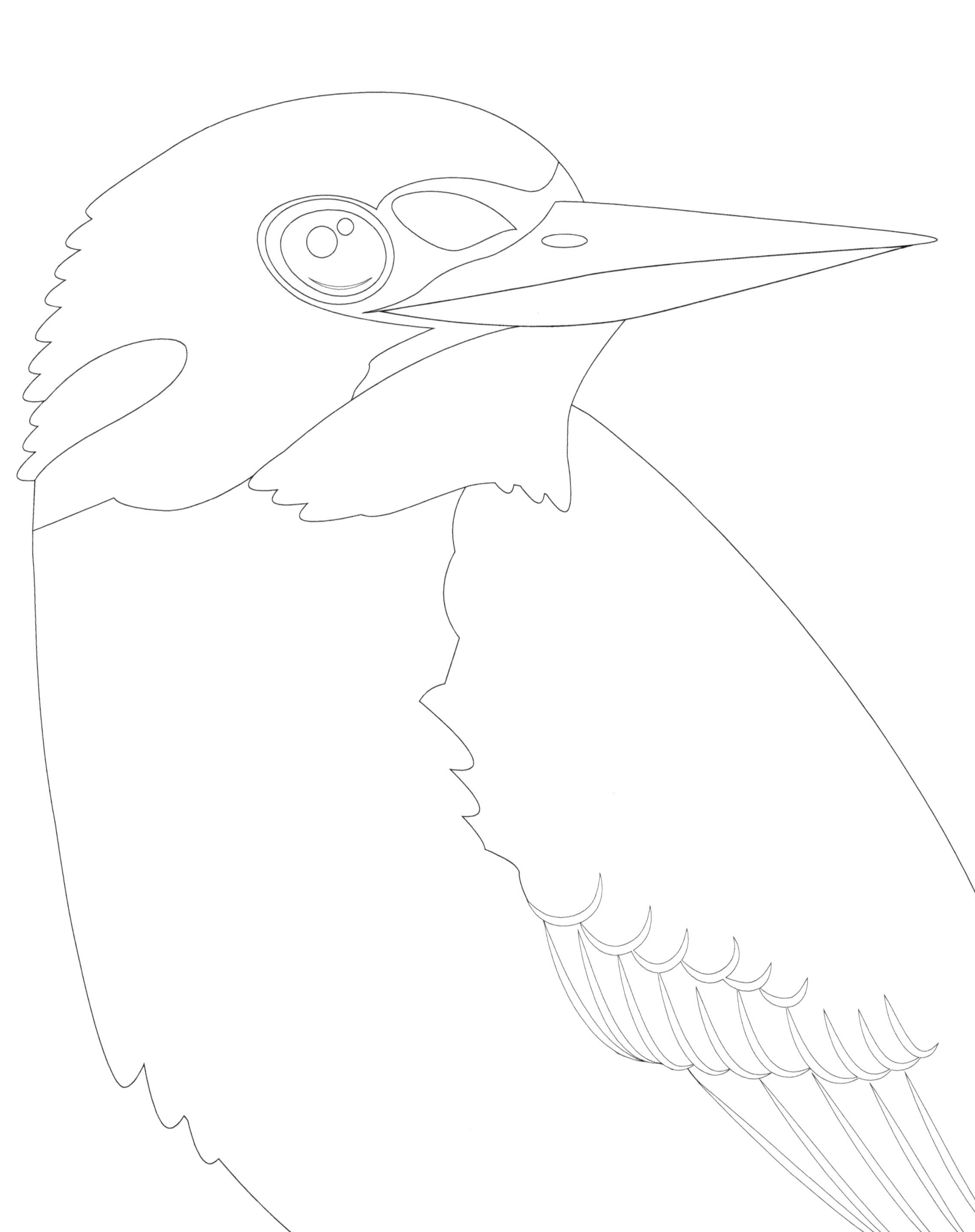

Laughing

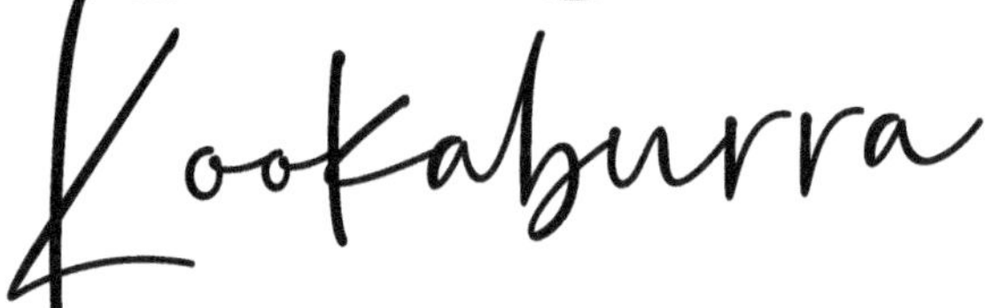

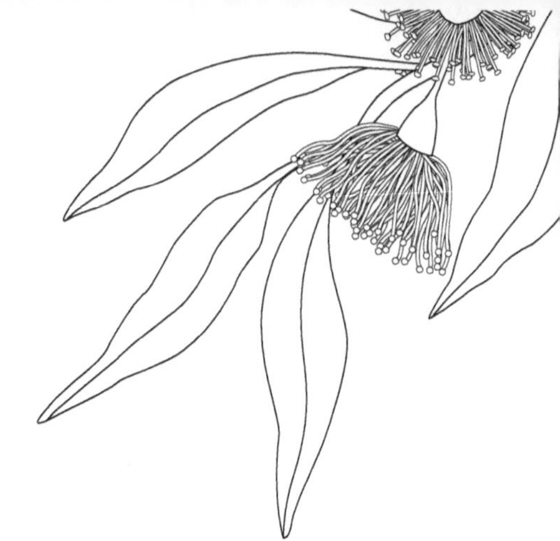

The Laughing Kookaburra's call is often described as a "laugh" because of its unique sound, which sounds like human laughter. However, Laughing Kookaburras are not laughing. Their call is used to mark their territory and warn other birds to stay away.

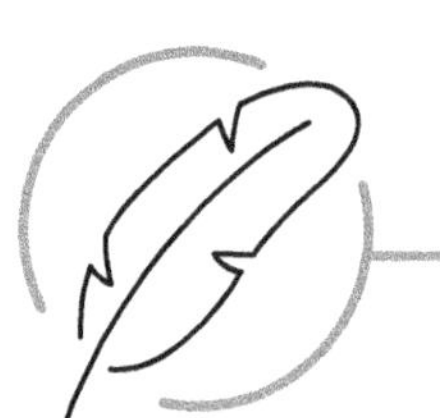

Identification

Laughing Kookaburras are recognisable by both their feathers and their voice. The feathers on their upper bodies and backs are brown, and their brown wings have patches of blue feathers. They have off-white undersides that are barred with dark brown. Their heads are off-white, with brown eye-stripes and they have large, dark curved beaks. Their tails are more broadly barred with light brown and black. They are one of the larger members of the Kingfisher family.

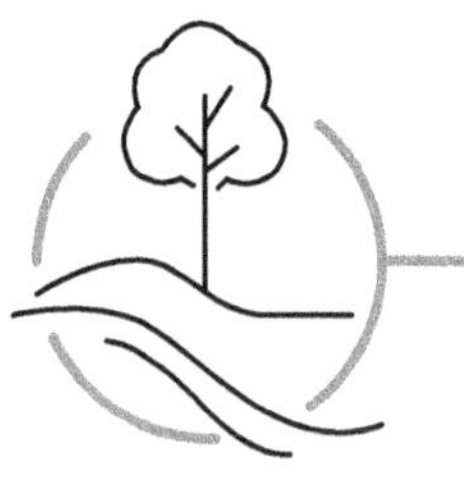

Habitat

Laughing Kookaburras are found in a variety of habitats throughout much of eastern and southern Australia, including Eucalyptus forests, woodlands, savannahs, and even suburban parks and gardens. They prefer areas with open ground for hunting their prey.

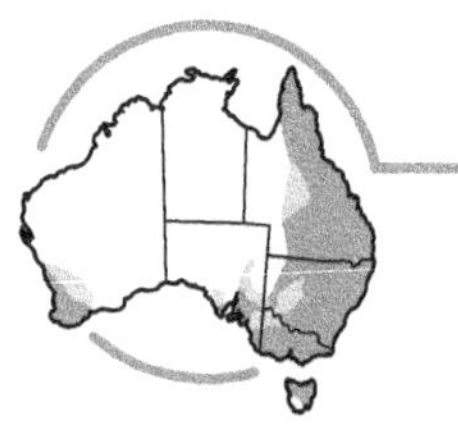

Distribution

Laughing Kookaburras are found throughout eastern Australia. They have been introduced to Tasmania and the south-west of Western Australia. Kookaburras are absent from the driest desert areas in the central part of the continent and the densest forests in the far south of the country.

Bird Journal

Date seen: ___________________ Time seen: ___________________

Location: ___________________

Observations: ___________________

____

____

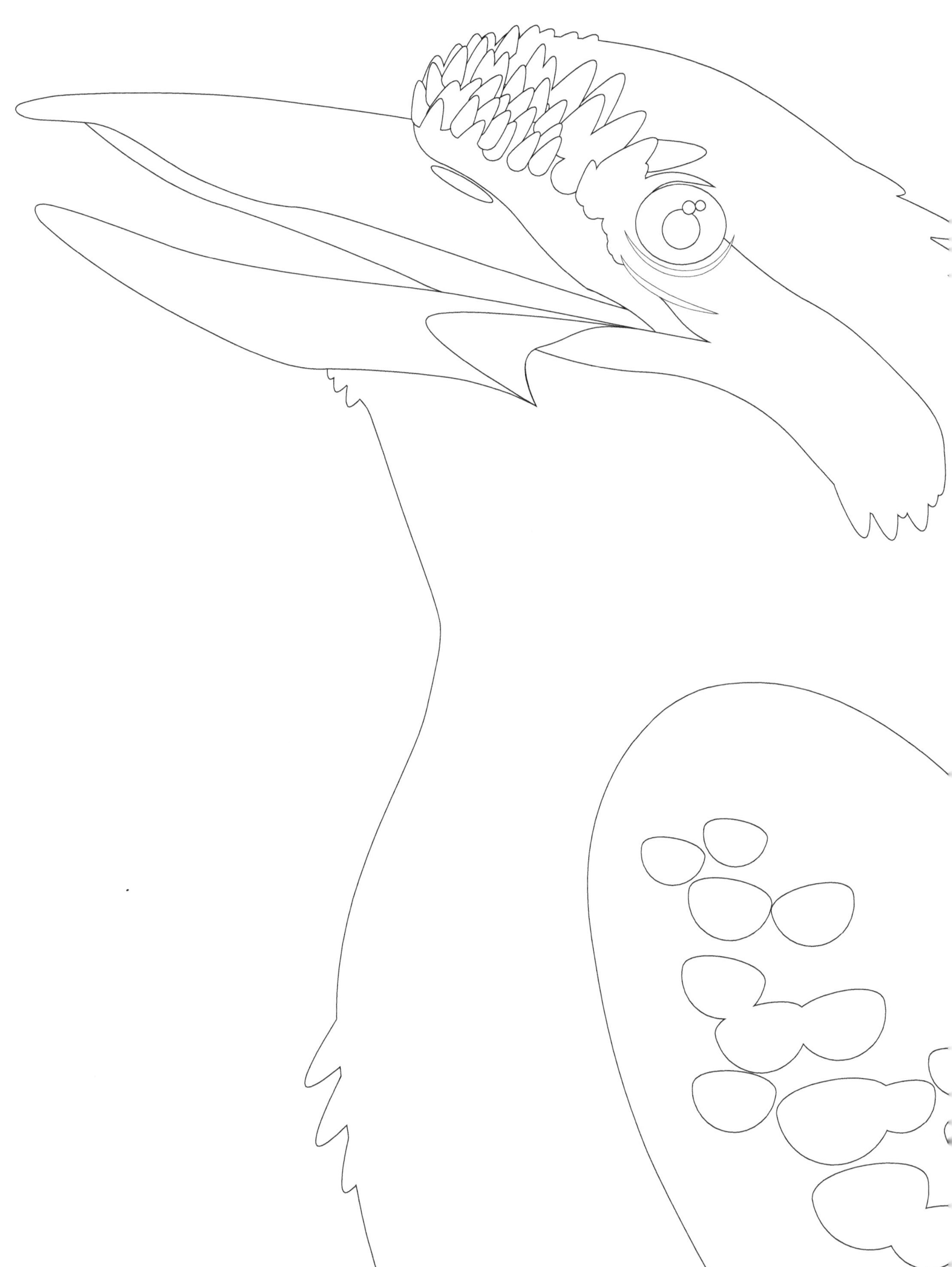

Rainbow Lorikeet

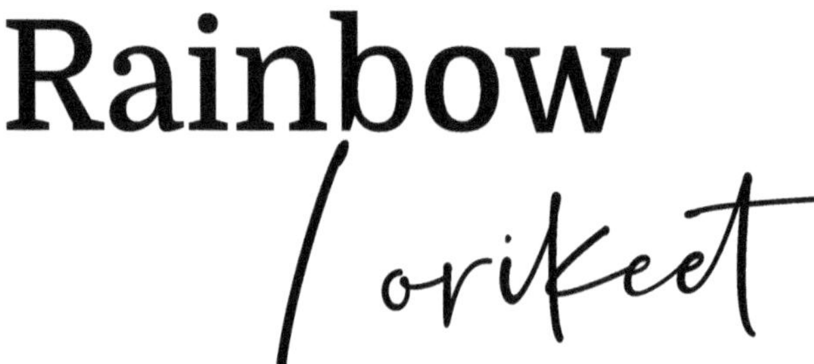
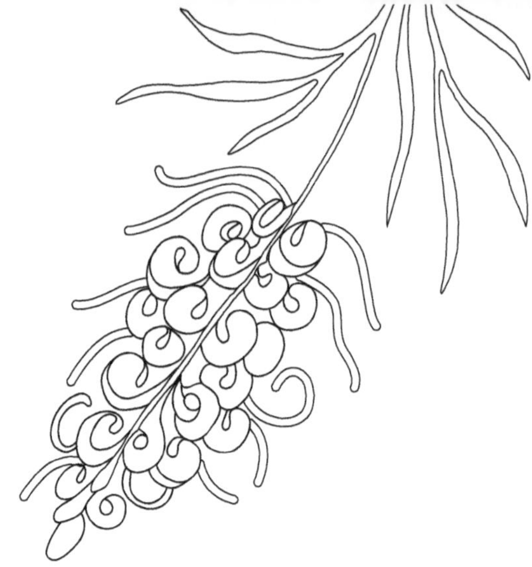

Rainbow Lorikeets eat nectar, pollen, and fruit, and have a special tongue for their unique diet. The tips of their tongues have small raised bumps that allow them to collect pollen and nectar from flowers.

Identification

Rainbow Lorikeets are eye-catching, characterised by their vibrant red beaks and colourful feathers. Both males and females have the same appearance: blue heads and bellies, green wings, backs, and tails, and orange or yellow chests. These birds often move in noisy flocks. They can be quite vocal, making loud screeches and squawks.

Habitat

Rainbow Lorikeets are found in a range of habitats, including rainforests, Eucalyptus forests, woodlands, and coastal grasslands. They are also found in urban and suburban areas, especially in parks and gardens with flowering trees and shrubs.

Distribution

Rainbow Lorikeets can be found throughout the eastern and south-eastern parts of Australia, including the coastal regions of Queensland, New South Wales, Victoria, and South Australia.

Bird Journal

Date seen: ______________________   Time seen: ______________________

Location: ______________________

Observations: ______________________

____

____

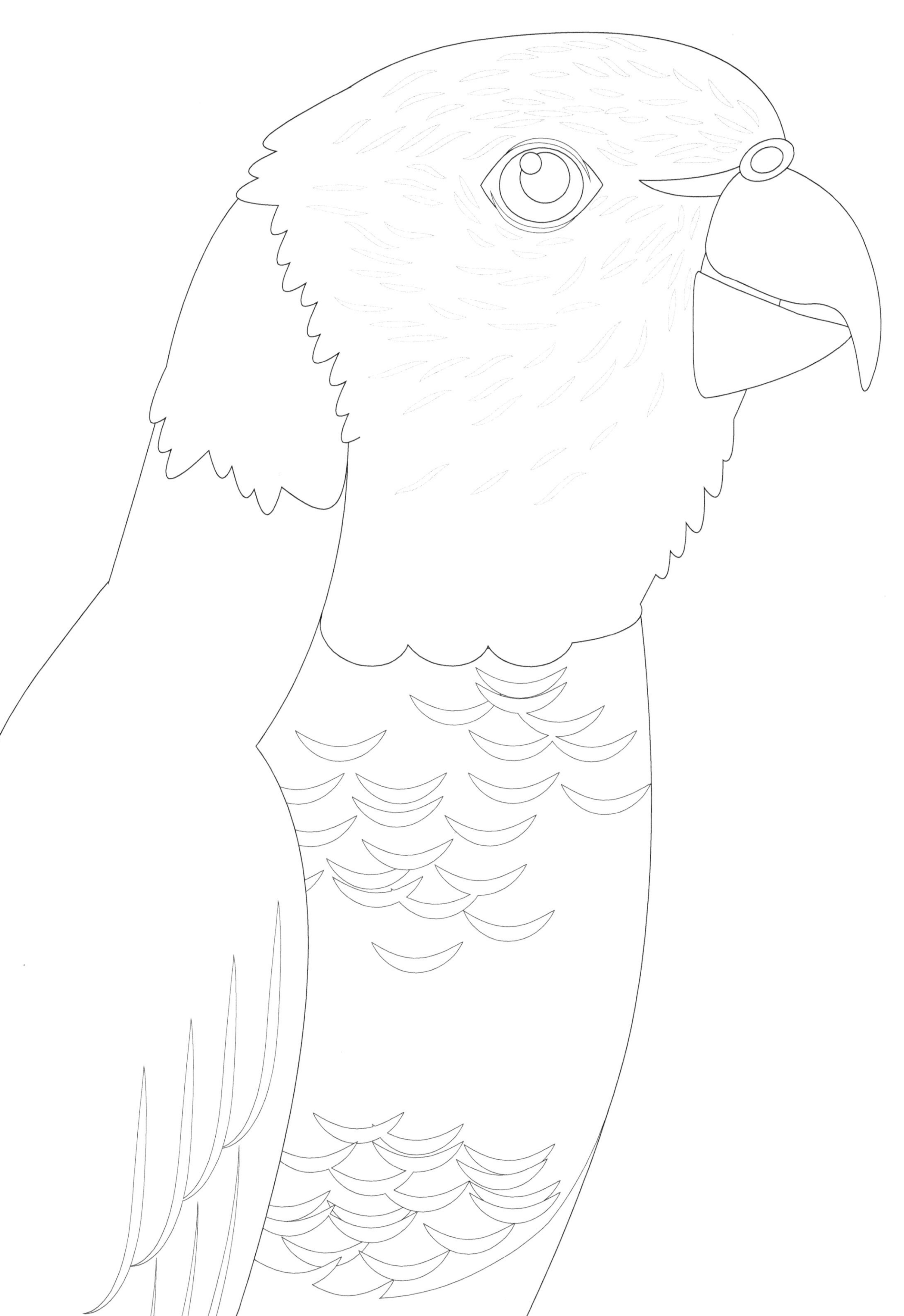

Superb

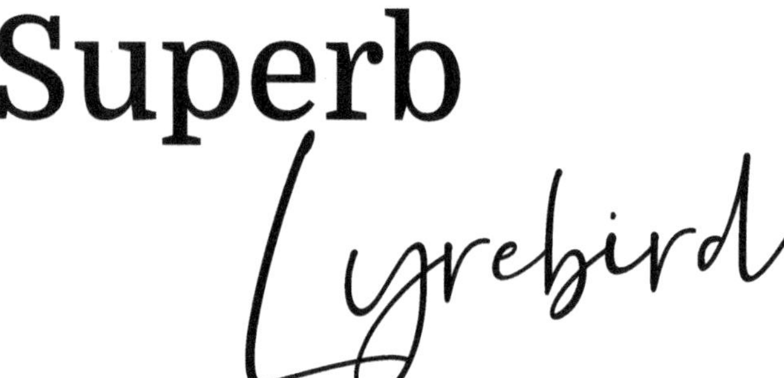

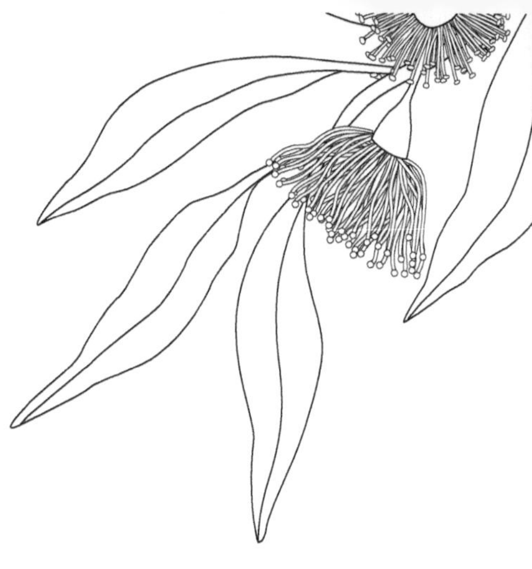

Superb Lyrebirds are known for their unusual ability to mimic a wide variety of sounds, including other birds, human speech and man-made sounds such as car alarms and chainsaws.

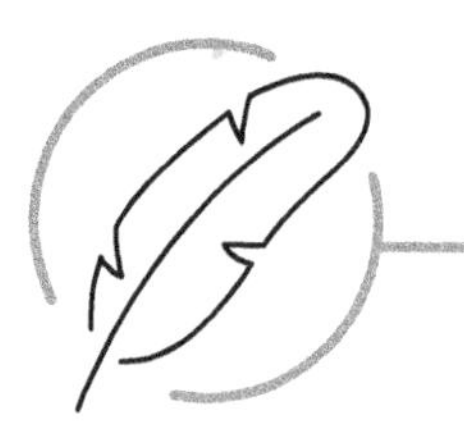

Identification

Superb Lyrebirds are large, ground-dwelling birds. Adult males have long, curved tail feathers that resemble the shape of a lyre, a stringed musical instrument. The males have patterns of spots and stripes trimming their tail feathers. They have dark brown feathers with lighter underbellies, reddish-brown wings and a prominent reddish-brown neck patches. Females and younger Lyrebirds have a duller appearance, with shorter tails that have no lyre-shaped feathers.

Habitat

Superb Lyrebirds live in a range of habitats, including rainforests, Eucalyptus forests, and scrublands in valleys of mountain regions. Superb Lyrebirds need areas with dense vegetation and a moist understory.

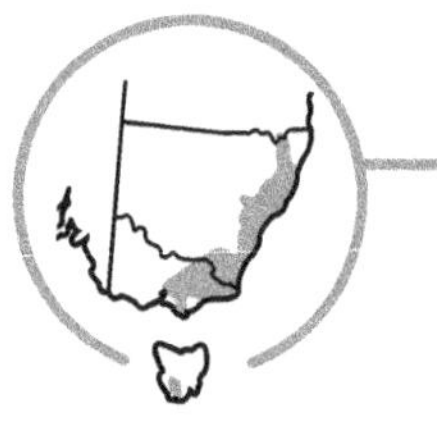

Distribution

Superb Lyrebirds are found in the eastern parts of Victoria, New South Wales, south-eastern Queensland and southern Tasmania.

Bird Journal

Date seen: **Time seen:**

Location:

Observations:

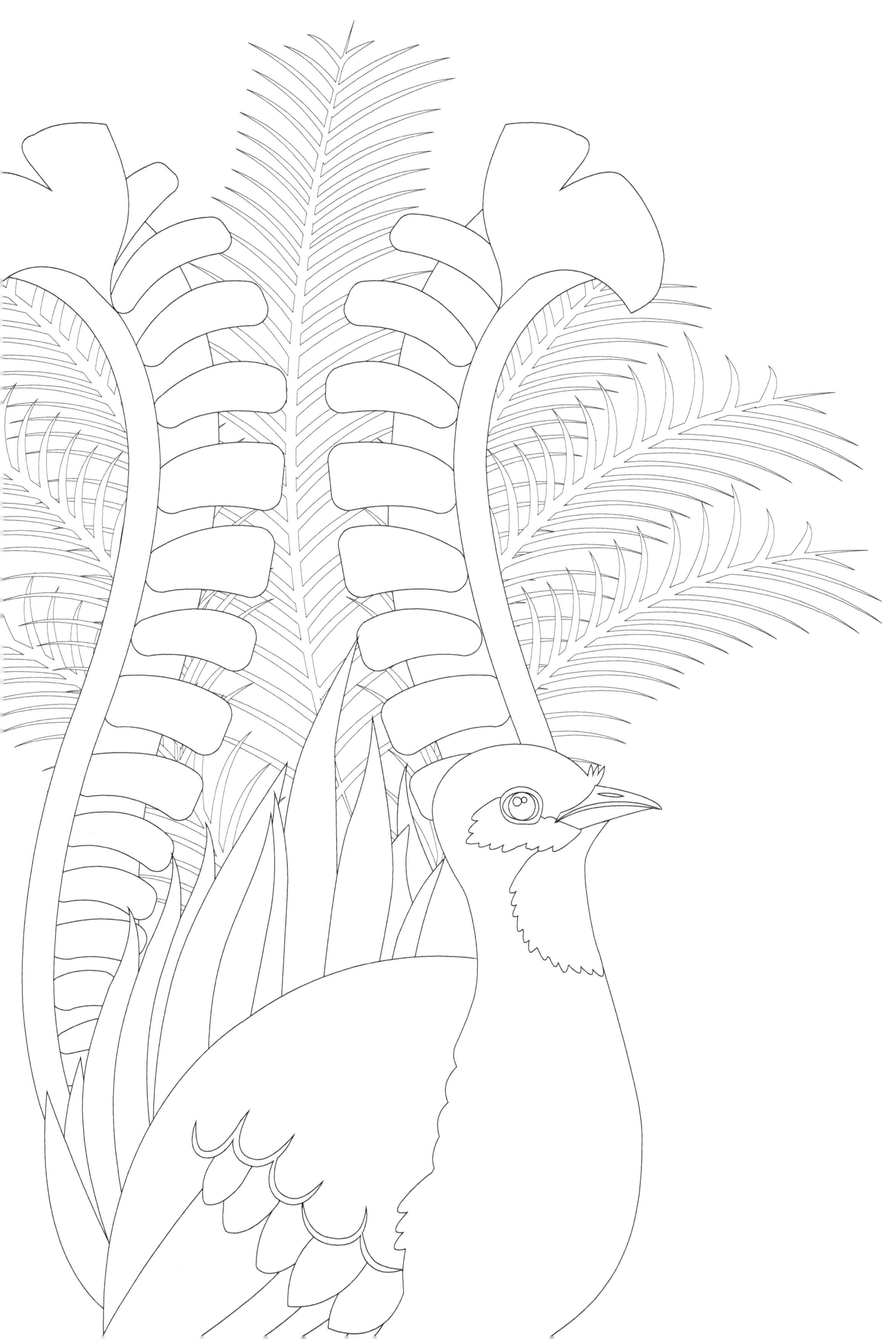

Australian
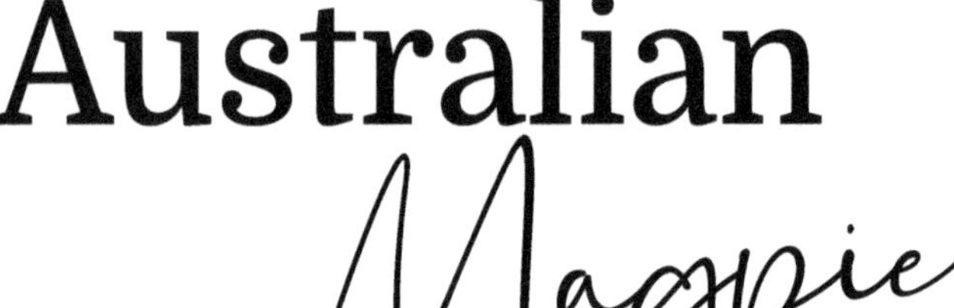

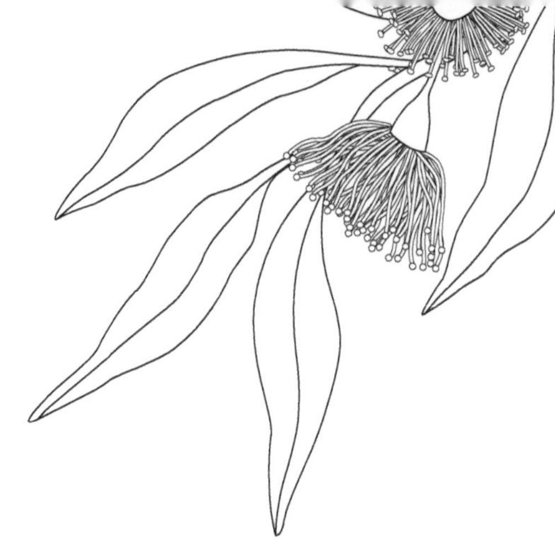

Magpies are one of Australia's most skilled songbirds. They are known for their varied calls, which range from warbling and trilling to musical notes, and the copying of other birds' songs.

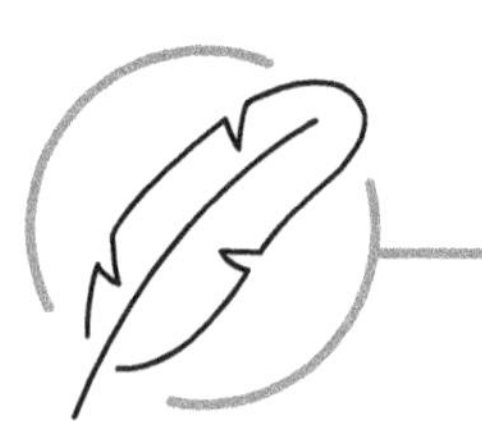

Identification

Australian Magpies have distinctive black and white feathers, but their feather patterns changes depending on their location. Across most of Australia, their necks, shoulders, and wing underparts are white, while their wings, backs, and tails are black. In the south-east, centre, south-west and Tasmania, their backs are entirely white. Females have the same feather patterns, but have grey necks. Adult birds have chestnut brown eyes.

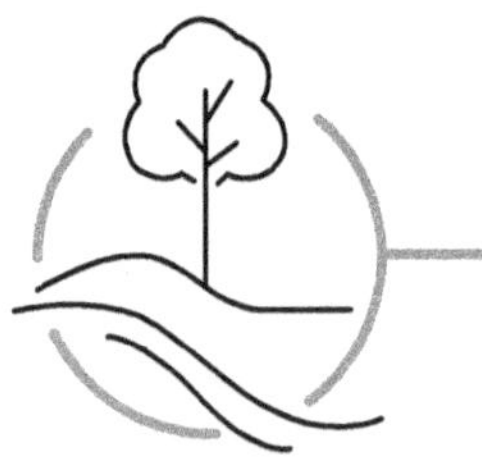

Habitat

Australian Magpies prefer habitats with some open ground for foraging, such as parks, gardens and golf courses. They are found in a range of habitats, including open forests, woodlands, grasslands, and scrublands. They are often near water sources, such as rivers, lakes, and wetlands.

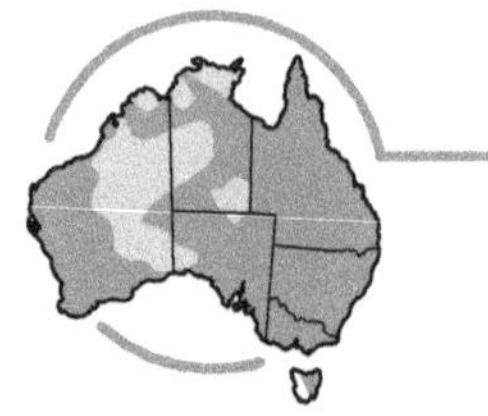

Distribution

Australian Magpies are found throughout most of Australia, except for the driest areas of the inland deserts.

Bird Journal

Date seen: _______________________   Time seen: _______________________

Location: ____

Observations: ____

____

____

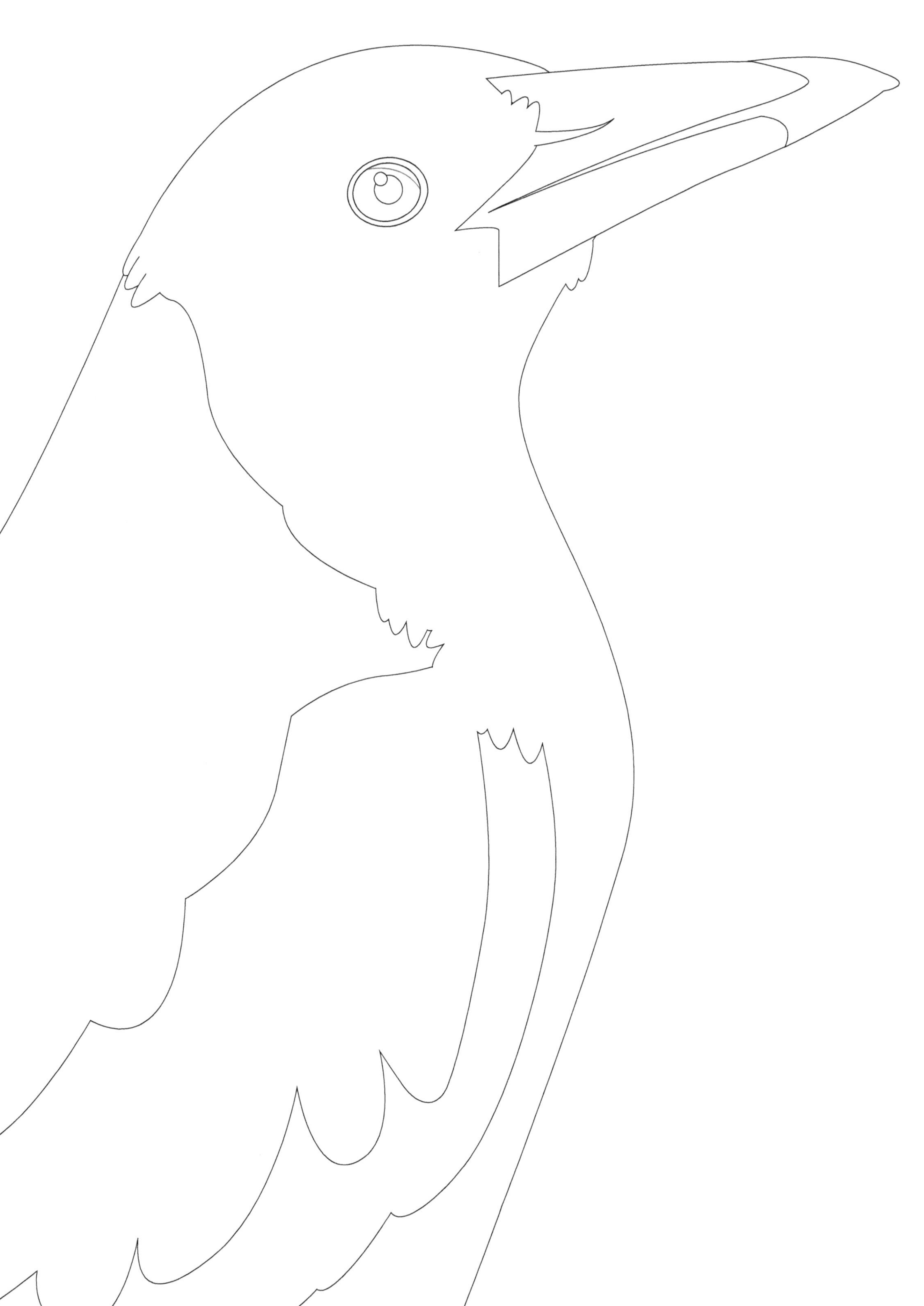

Eastern Barn Owl

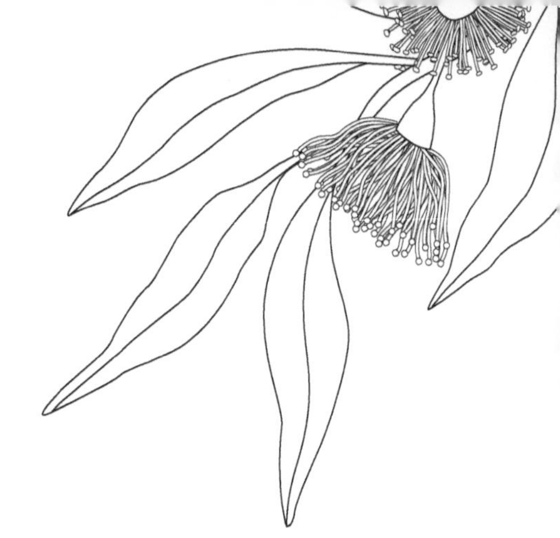

Eastern Barn Owls have a unique heart-shaped facial disc that helps them to direct sound waves to their ears and locate their prey in the dark. Their facial discs are also a way of communicating. They can change the shape of their disc to show emotions to other owls.

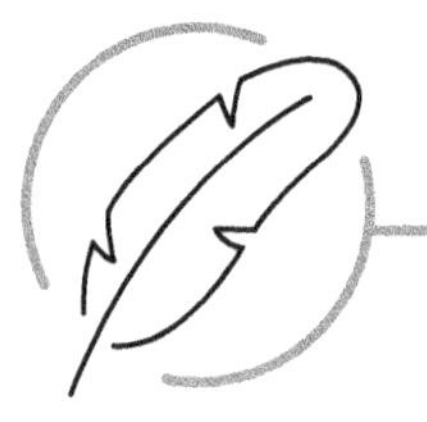

Identification

Eastern Barn Owls are most active at night. Their facial discs are white, which contrasts with their sandy orange and light grey backs and wings. Both their backs and breasts are spotted with black. They have long legs and short tails with brown and grey feathers. Their eyes are dark, and they have hooked beaks that are well-suited for prey. Eastern Barn Owls have a silent flight because the shape of their wings and feathers help to muffle sound.

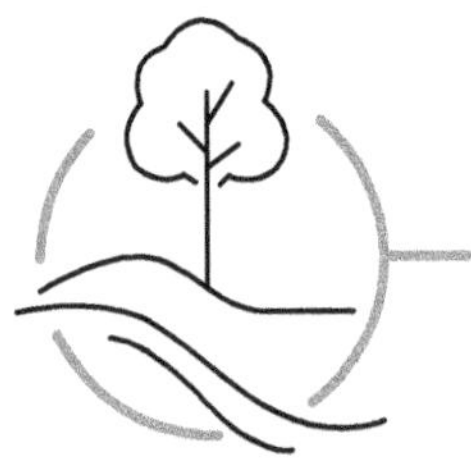

Habitat

Eastern Barn Owls can be found in a variety of habitats throughout Australia. They prefer open grasslands, agricultural fields, and savannahs with scattered trees, but can also be found in suburban and urban areas, as well as forested regions. Eastern Barn Owls require open areas to hunt.

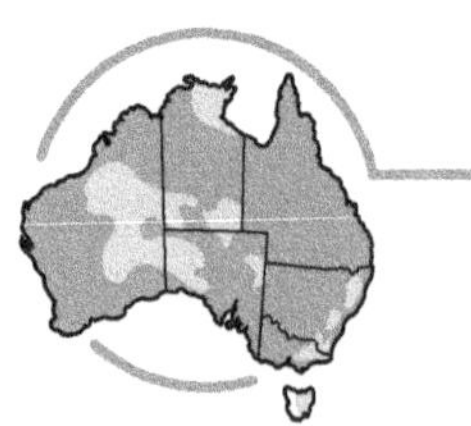

Distribution

Eastern Barn Owls are found in every state and territory of Australia, from the tropical north to the temperate south. Their distribution is limited only by habitat and food availability.

Bird Journal

Date seen: _______________________   Time seen: _______________________

Location: _______________________

Observations: _______________________

____

____

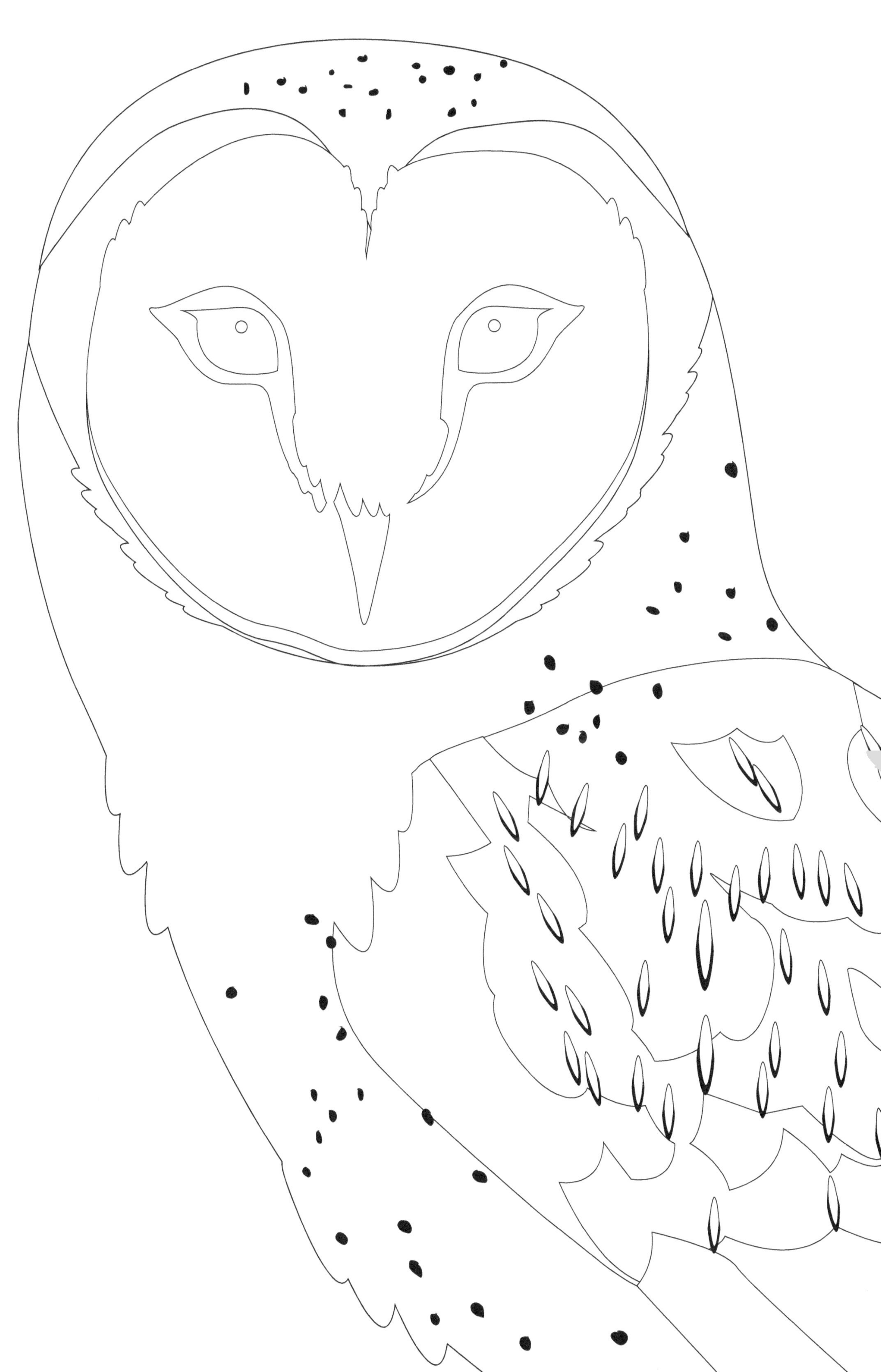

Australian *Pelican*

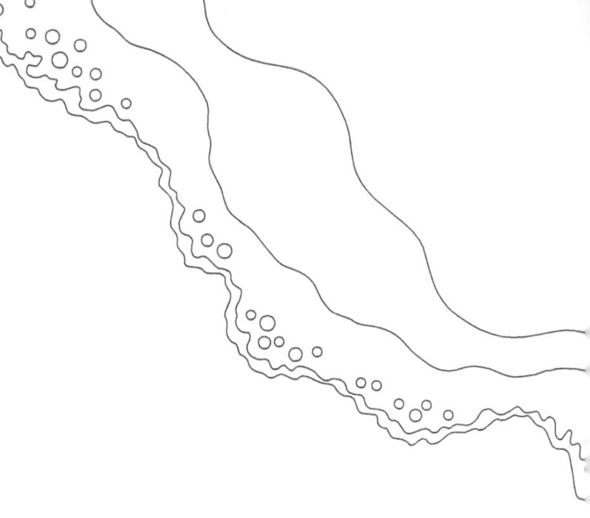

Australian Pelicans are known for their beaks, they are long, broad, and have a large expandable pouch, known as the gular sac. The gular sac can hold up to 13 litres of water.

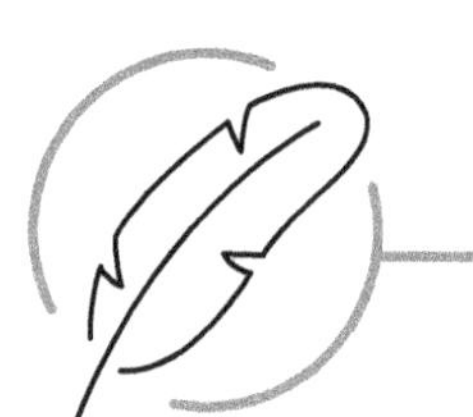

Identification

Australian Pelicans are recognisable because of their size and unique features. They are one of the largest waterbirds in the world, with wingspans of 2.5 metres. They have white plumage, with black feathers on their wings, and long, pink tinged beaks that measure 40cm - 50cm. Males are larger and have larger beaks than females.

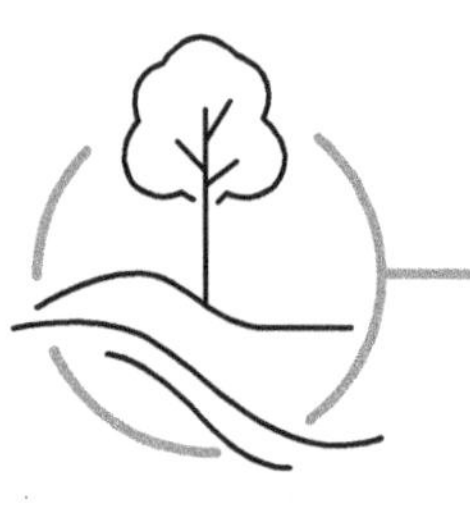

Habitat

Australian Pelicans are found in a wide range of aquatic habitats, including rivers, lakes, estuaries, and coastal waters. Pelicans prefer habitats with shallow water and areas of open water, where they can find fish and other aquatic prey. They are also found in wetlands, lagoons, and saltwater bays. These birds can thrive in both freshwater and saltwater environments.

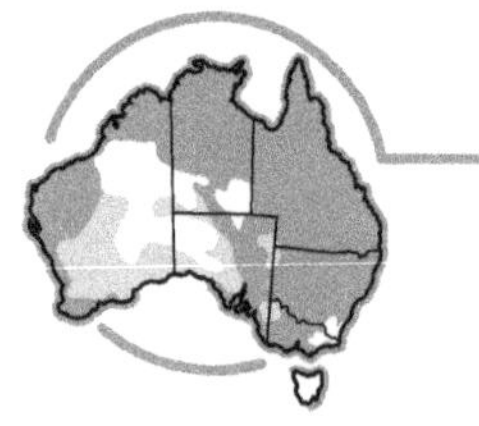

Distribution

Australian Pelicans are found throughout most of Australia, except for the inland deserts.

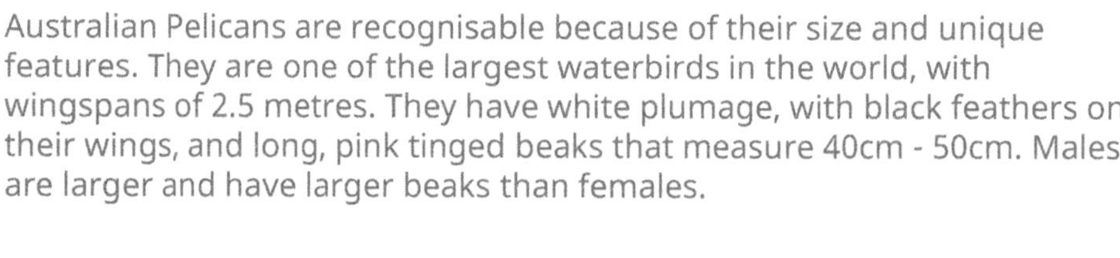

Bird Journal

Date seen: ______________________   Time seen: ______________________

Location: ____

Observations: ____

____

____

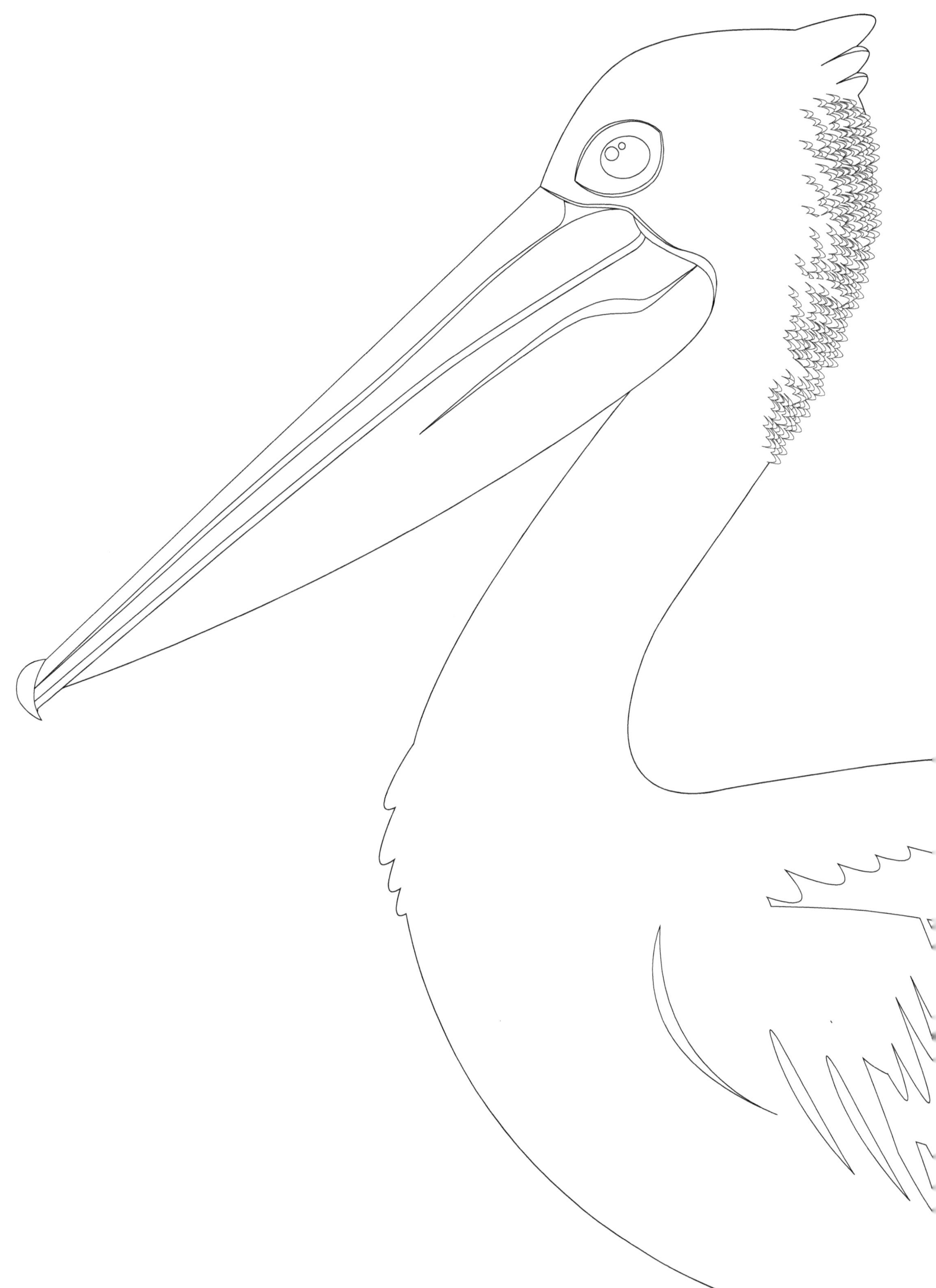

Little *Penguin*

Little Penguins are excellent swimmers and can spend weeks away at sea. They dive up to 60 metres in search of small fish, squid, and krill.

Identification

Little Penguins are the smallest species of penguin and grow about 33cm tall, weighing around 1kg. They have blue-grey heads and backs with white fronts and pale pink feet with black edging. Their flippers are darker with a white edge. Little Penguins have short tails and small, pointed beaks.

Habitat

Little Penguins live in a range of coastal and offshore habitats. They are found in areas with rocky or sandy shorelines, where they can seek shelter in rocky crevices. They require access to clean water, as they spend much of their time swimming and diving, looking for fish and other small marine creatures. Little Penguins breed in large colonies on offshore islands, where they are protected from predators such as foxes. These colonies are in areas with suitable nesting sites, such as rocky outcrops or areas with dense vegetation.

Distribution

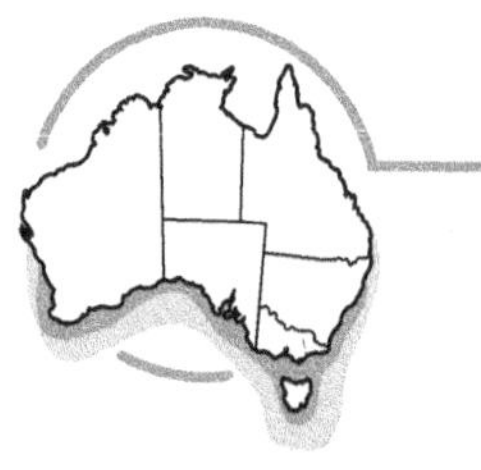

Little Penguins are found along the southern coastline, from Western Australia to New South Wales, including Tasmania.

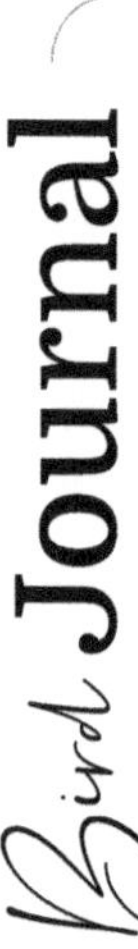

Date seen: _______________   Time seen: _______________

Location: _______________

Observations: _______________

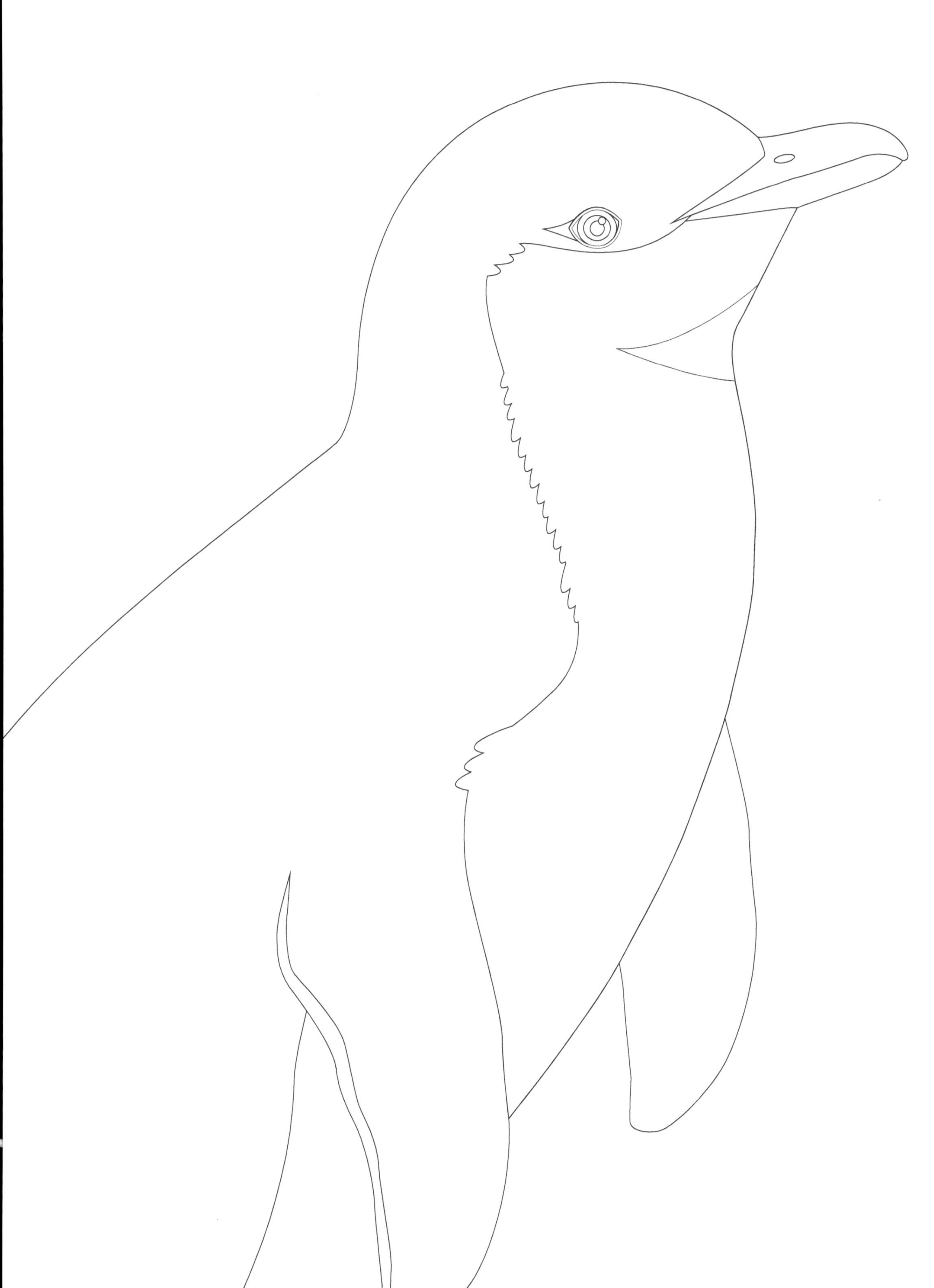

Eastern *Rosella*

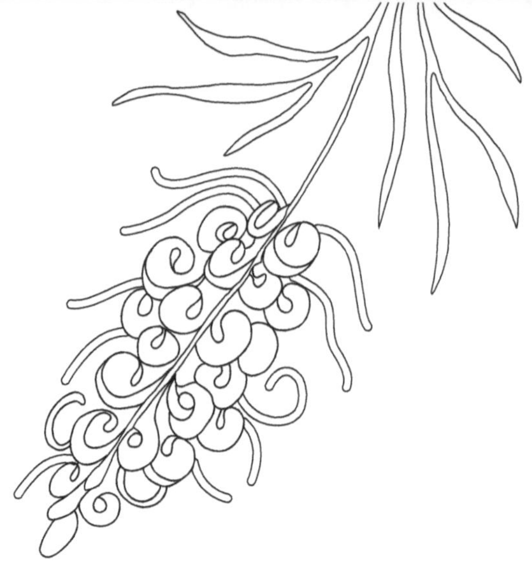

Eastern Rosellas fly in a gentle up-and-down movement, often flying close to the ground. When landing on trees, they glide upwards and spread their tails out like a fan.

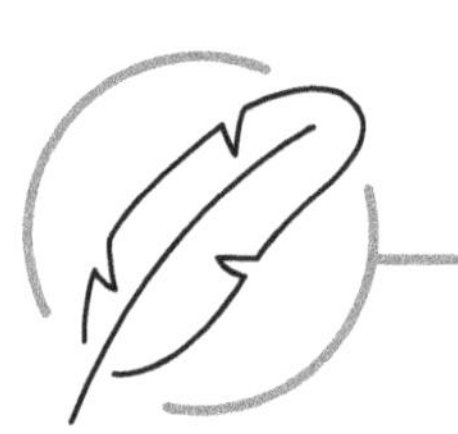

Identification

Eastern Rosellas have distinctive red heads, white cheeks and yellow to greenish upper bodies. Their wings are black and blue with yellow and green markings, and their tails are blue and green with red highlights. Their beaks are off-white and their legs are grey. Young birds are duller and have yellow or orange beaks, which change to off-white when they mature.

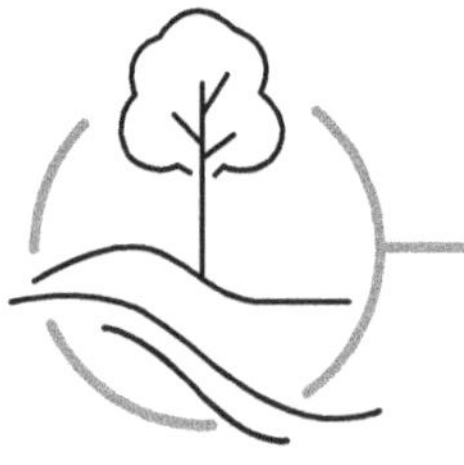

Habitat

Eastern Rosellas are found in a range of habitats, including forests, woodlands, parks, and gardens. They prefer habitats with a mix of trees and grassy areas, and are found near water sources.

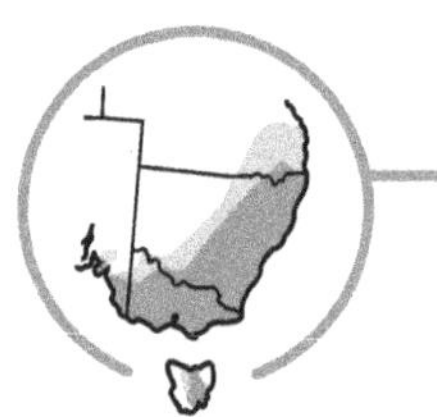

Distribution

Eastern Rosellas are found in eastern and south-eastern Australia, from southern Queensland to South Australia, Tasmania, and Victoria. They also occur in parts of south-eastern New South Wales.

Bird Journal

Date seen: Time seen:

Location:

Observations:

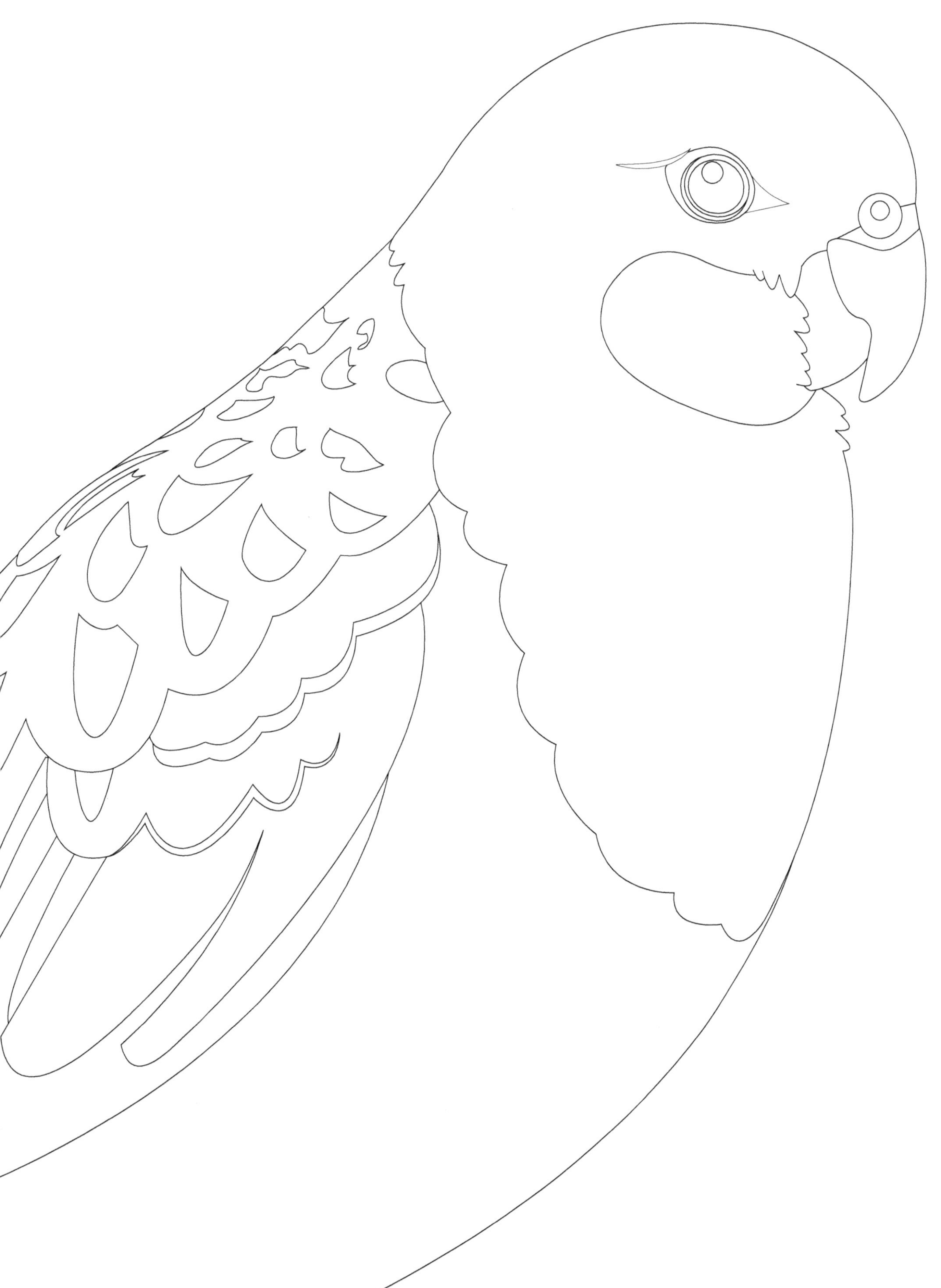

Silver Gull

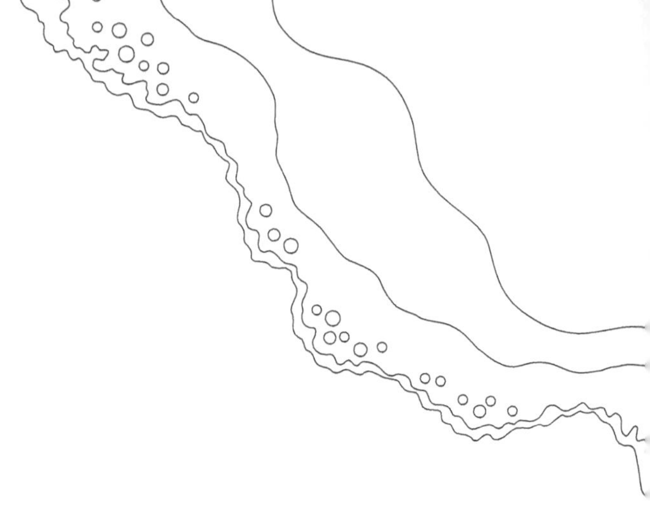

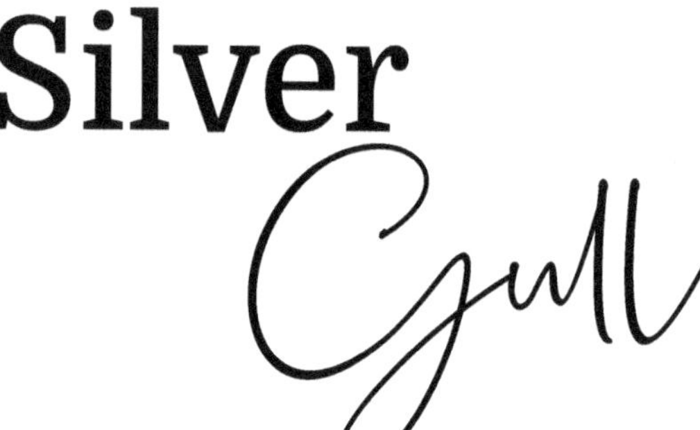

Silver Gulls, also known as Seagulls, are successful scavengers, pestering humans for scraps and stealing unattended food.

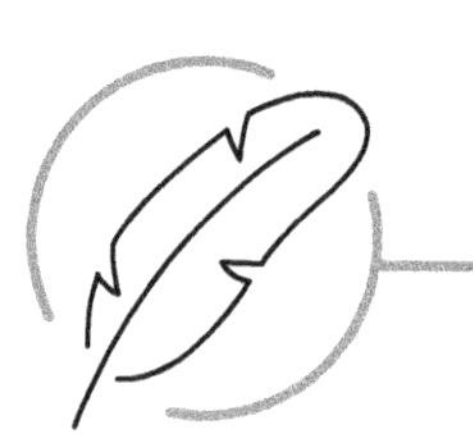

Identification

Silver Gulls have white heads, necks and bodies, with light grey on their backs. Their wings are grey and have black tips. Their beaks, legs and eye-rings are bright orange-red in adult birds. Young Silver Gulls have brown and white mottled feathers which change to their adult feathers by their second year.

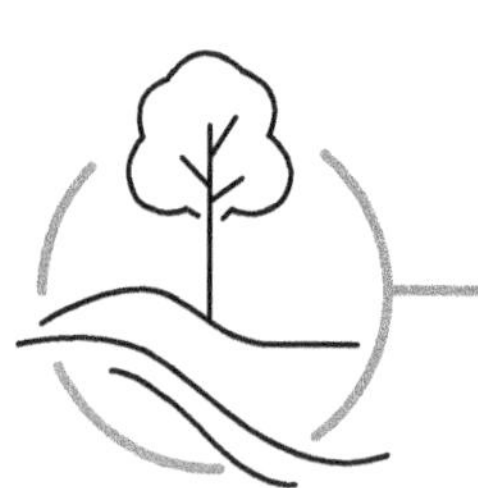

Habitat

Silver Gulls are an adaptable bird found in a range of habitats, including coastal areas, beaches, islands, parks, and urban environments. They are found in cities and towns, often gathering in large flocks around parks, beaches, and rubbish tips where they have easy access to food.

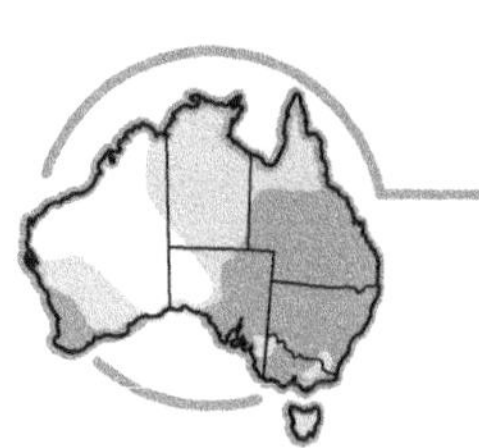

Distribution

Silver Gulls are found throughout Australia, including the mainland and nearby coastal areas. Their widespread distribution and ability to adapt have made them one of the most common and well-known seabirds in Australia.

Bird Journal

Date seen: Time seen:

Location:

Observations:

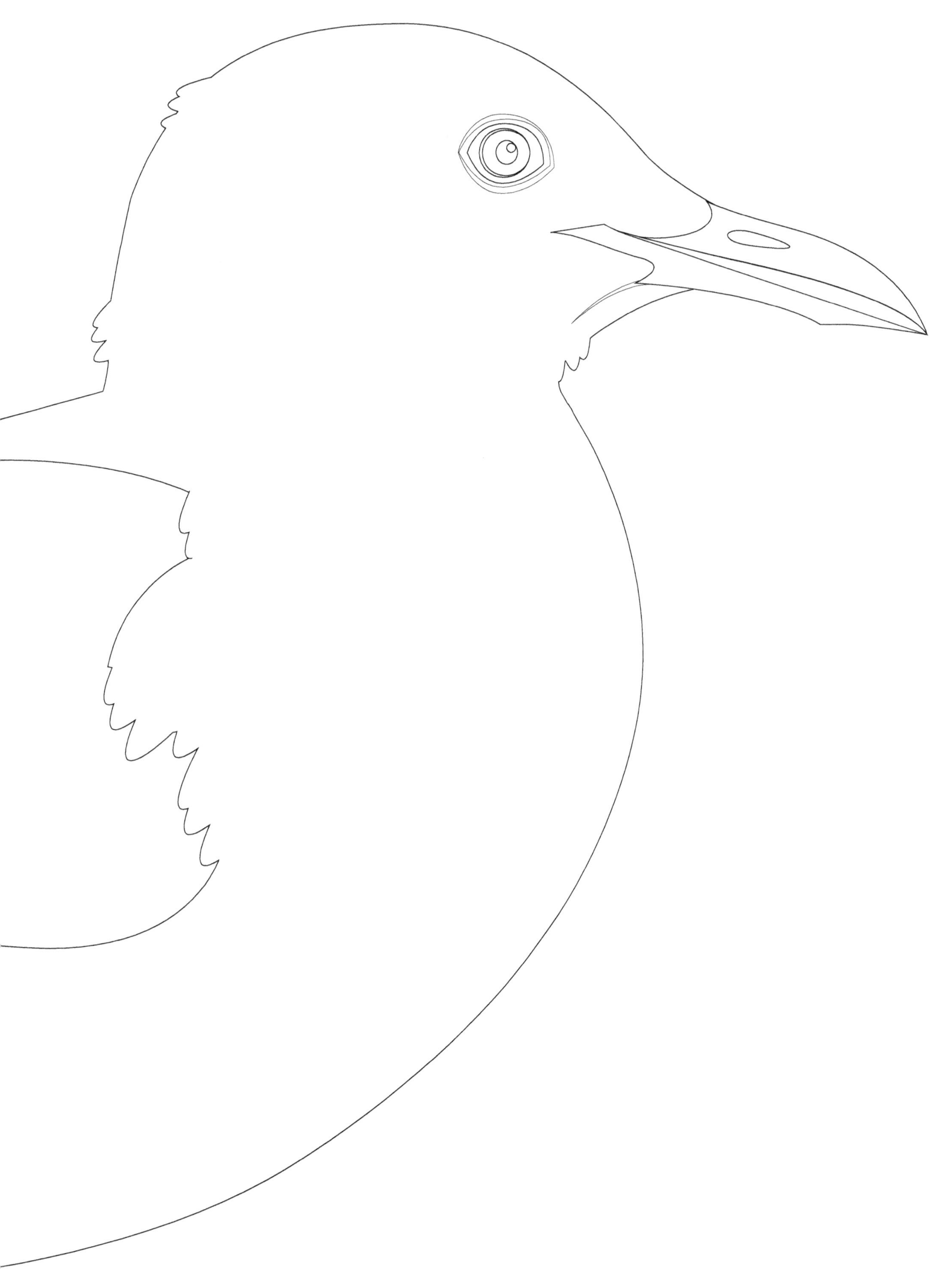

Black *Swan*

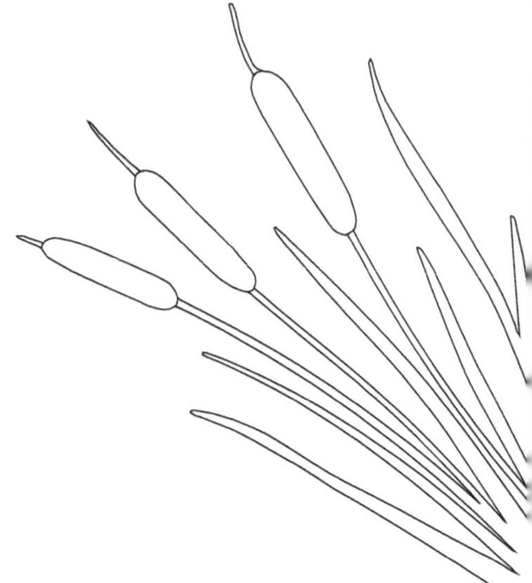

Black Swans are unique as they are the only species of swan that displays entirely black feathers. They also have the longest neck of all swan species.

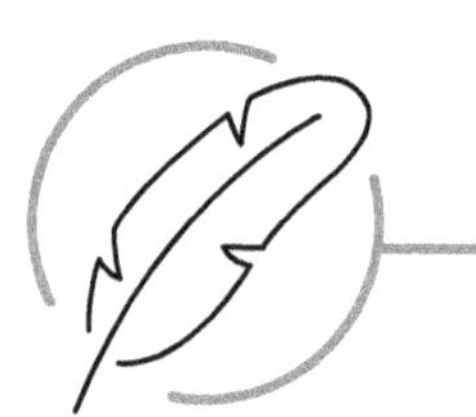

Identification

Black Swans are completely black, except for their broad white wingtips that are visible during flight. The Black Swan's two metre wing span makes a whistling sound in flight. They have orange-red bills with a pale tip and a narrow white band towards the end. They have long s-curved necks and distinctive red eyes. Younger black swans are greyer and have black wingtips. Females are smaller than males.

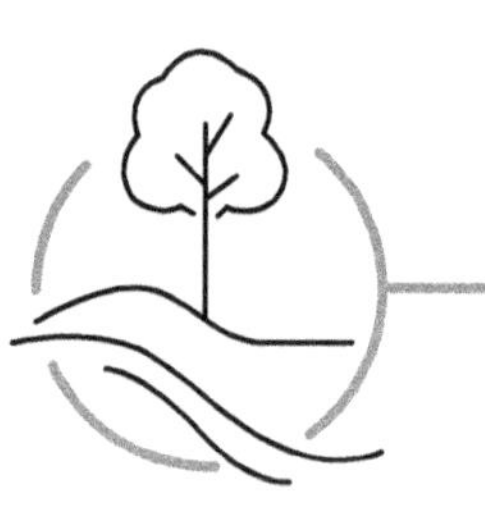

Habitat

Black Swans inhabit a variety of wetland habitats, including lakes, rivers, estuaries, and coastal bays. They require a distance of 40 metres or more of water to take off in flight. Black Swans prefer shallow water with vegetation for feeding and nesting. They can also be found in brackish or saltwater environments.

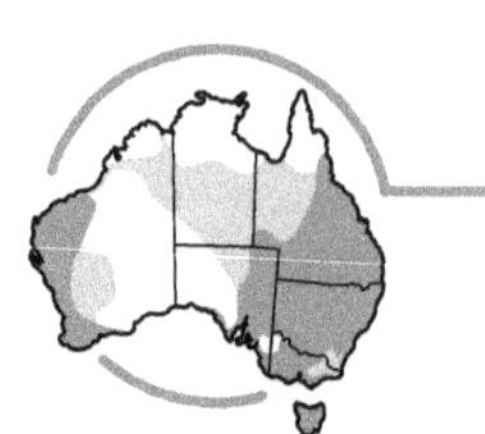

Distribution

Black Swans are found throughout all Australian states. They are most common in the southern and western parts of the country, but can be found in eastern and northern regions.

Bird Journal

Date seen: ___________________   **Time seen:** ___________________

Location: ___________________

Observations: ___________________

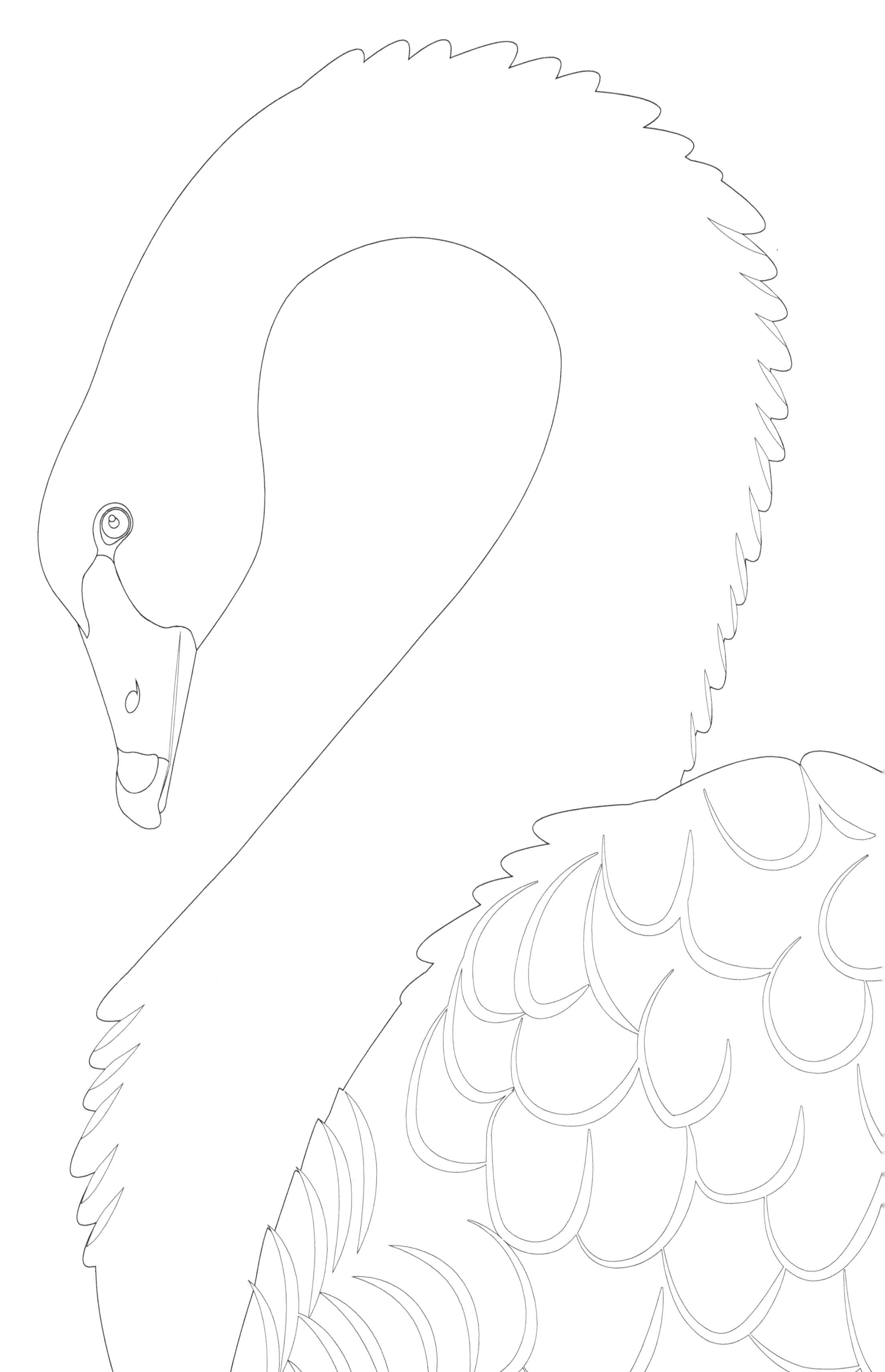

Draw your own birds

Bird:

Date seen:

Time seen:

Location:

Observations:

Bird:

Date seen:

Time seen:

Location:

Observations:

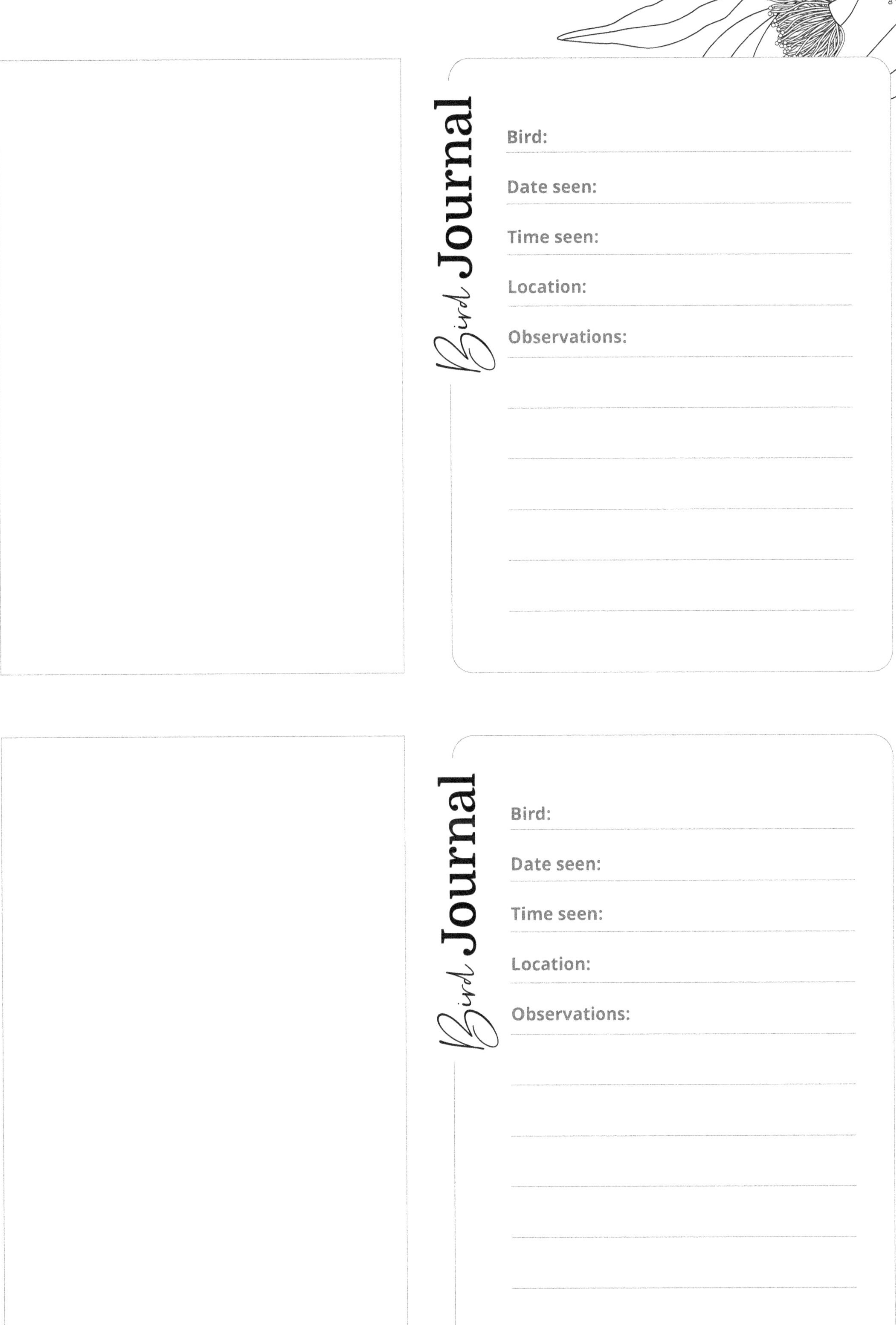

Bird Journal

Bird:
Date seen:
Time seen:
Location:
Observations:

Bird Journal

Bird:
Date seen:
Time seen:
Location:
Observations:

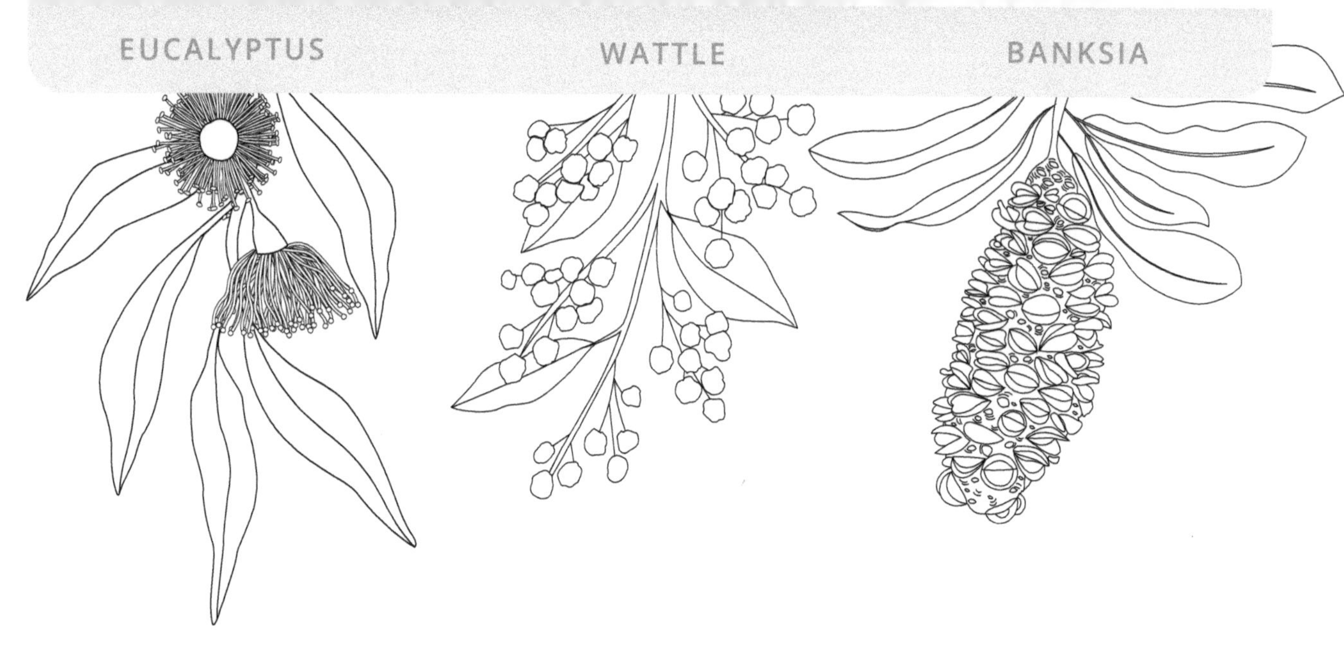

Australian flora

Inside this colouring book, you'll find a collection of Australian flora that attract a variety of Australian birds. These flowers & trees provide both shelter and nourishment to our feathered friends.

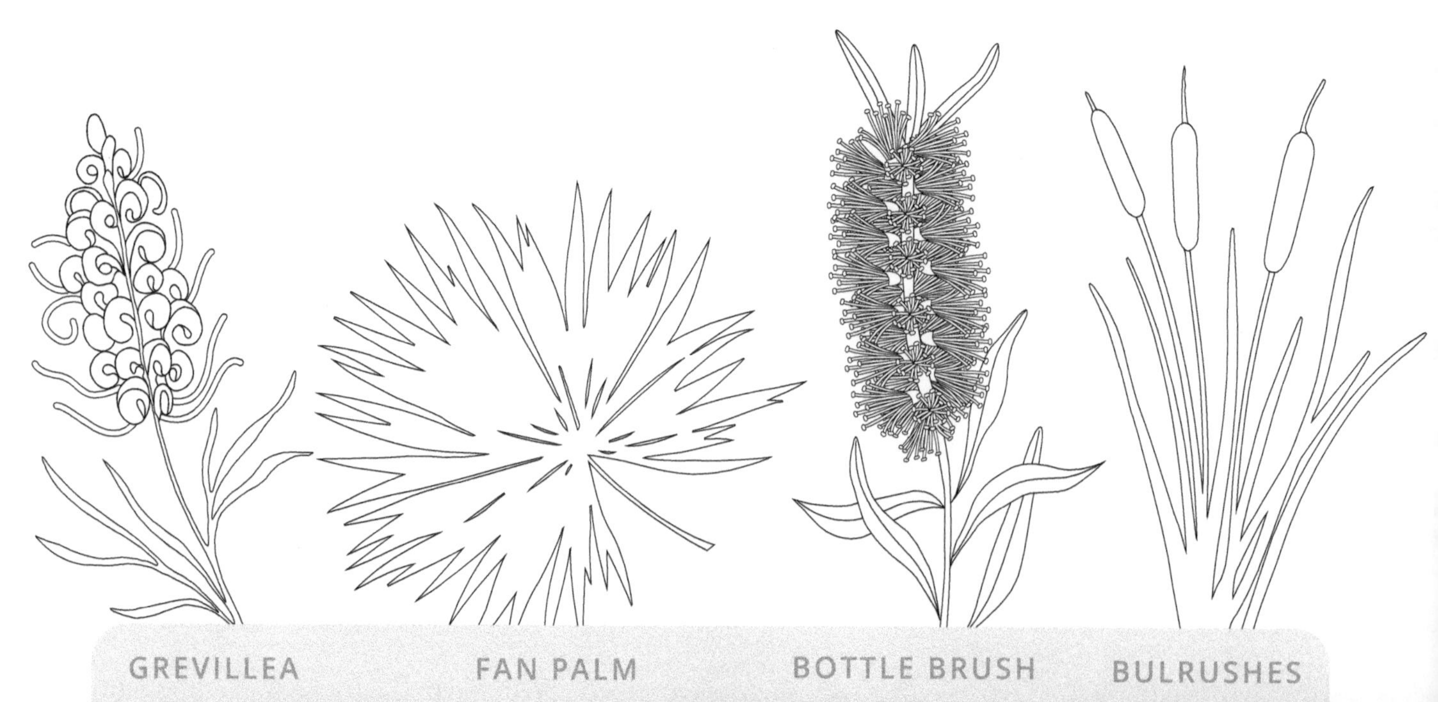

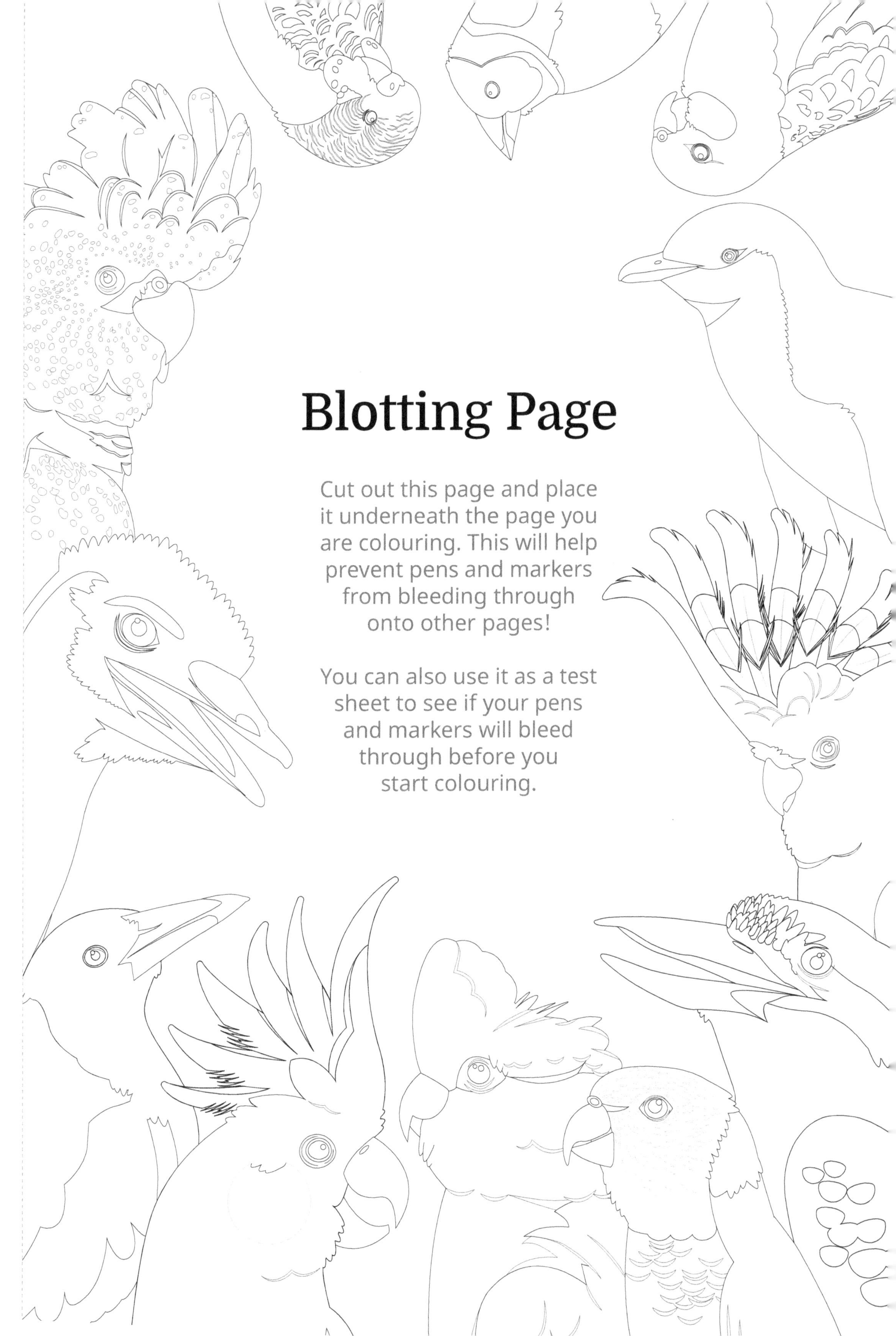

Blotting Page

Cut out this page and place it underneath the page you are colouring. This will help prevent pens and markers from bleeding through onto other pages!

You can also use it as a test sheet to see if your pens and markers will bleed through before you start colouring.